Peter Raina (ed.)

A.V. Dicey
General Characteristics of English Constitutionalism

Six Unpublished Lectures

PETER LANG
Oxford • Bern • Berlin • Bruxelles • Frankfurt am Main • New York • Wien

Bibliographic information published by Die Deutsche Bibliothek
Die Deutsche Bibliothek lists this publication in the Deutsche Nationalbibliografie; detailed bibliographic data is available on the Internet at <http://dnb.ddb.de>.

A catalogue record for this book is available from The British Library.

Library of Congress Cataloging-in-Publication Data:

Dicey, Albert Venn, 1835-1922
A.V. Dicey : general characteristics of English constitutionalism : six unpublished lectures / Peter Raina.
p. cm.
Includes bibliographical references and index.
ISBN 978-3-03911-955-4 (alk. paper)
1. Constitutional law--England. I. Raina, Peter K., 1935- II. Title.
KD3989.D527 2009
342.4202--dc22
2009017883

Cover image: Albert Venn Dicey (1835–1922), by Désiré François Laugée, 1872.
Courtesy of the President and Fellows of Trinity College, Oxford.
Cover design: Mette Bundgaard, Peter Lang Ltd
ISBN 978-3-03911-955-4

Hochfeldstrasse 32, CH-3012 Bern, Switzerland
info@peterlang.com, www.peterlang.com, www.peterlang.net

Printed in Germany

Contents

Preface

In the preface to the first edition (1985) of their book *The Changing Constitution* (now in its sixth edition) Professors Jeffrey Jowell and Dawn Oliver observe[1] that Albert Venn Dicey's *Introduction to the Study of the Law of the Constitution* (1885) had dominated British constitutional law and political theory for over one hundred years. And the fact is that Dicey's notions on the virtues of an unwritten constitution and on the supremacy of the UK Parliament still influence political discussion among constitutional historians. And yet, we are convinced that Dicey's text even today serves as a 'surrogate written constitution'. Dicey's own work was highly original and yet he fully acknowledges his inspiration by Paley as well as his gratitude to Blackstone,[2] Hallam,[3] Hearn[4] and Gardiner.[5] Not a page, writes Dicey, 'could have been written without reference' to these writers. But then Dicey developed his own hierarchy of principles to demonstrate his interpretation of the rule of law or the significance of the British Constitution.

Dicey won over several constitutional historians of his time to his views. However, the most serious critical remarks on Dicey's analysis of the rule of law were delivered by William Robson in his book *Justice and Administrative Law*, which appeared in 1928, six years after Dicey's death. Another major criticism followed when Sir Ivor Jennings wrote *The Law*

1 Jeffrey Jowell & Dawn Oliver, *The Changing Constitution* (Oxford, 2007).

2 Sir William Blackstone (1723–80), legal writer and historian; his major work: *Commentaries on the Laws of England* (4 vols, Oxford, 1765).

3 Henry Hallam (1777–1859), historian; major work: *The Constitutional History of England from the Accession of Henry VII to the Death of George II* (2 vols, London, 1827).

4 William Hearn (1826–88), legal and economic writer; major work: *The Government of England, its Structure and its Development* (London, 1867).

5 Samuel Gardiner (1829–1902), historian; major work: *Constitutional Documents of the Puritan Revolution* (London, 1899).

and the Constitution in 1933. In our own times Dicey's views are variously interpreted by distinguished constitutional historians. Professor P.P. Craig explains at length how important it is to understand that Dicey 'based his view of administrative law on a certain view of democracy, which can be termed unitary'.[6] An excellent and penetrating evaluation of Dicey's work and of his supporters and fervent critics has been rendered by Professor Jeffrey Jowell in his essay 'Dicey's Rule of Law: its critics and supporters'.[7] This essay is so well documented that we feel that any further discussion on the Diceyan rule of law would be superfluous.

Dicey's views on the rule of law and his interpretation of the British constitutional arrangements were judged entirely on his principal study, *Introduction to the Study of the Law of the Constitution*. Enough has already been written on this book. What concerns us chiefly are Dicey's diverse views, especially on the general characteristics of British constitutionalism, which are not sufficiently dealt with in his major published work.

In the late 1890s Dicey delivered a series of lectures at Oxford and Harvard universities on the English Party System, Characteristics of English Constitutionalism, Comparisons between English and other Executives (Parliamentary and non-Parliamentary Executives), the Cromwellian Constitution, English Constitutionalism under George III and Party Government. These lectures have so far remained unpublished. They further reveal Dicey's distinguished mind. His thoughts are enlightening, his knowledge is profound, and there is great acuteness in what he analyses. There is less speculation in his articulation, more practical thinking in his intentions. Dicey might have been a controversial political figure in so far as his orthodox Liberalism and his opposition to home rule for Ireland are concerned, but he was certainly a rational and pragmatic scholar, searching to find the way to apply constitutional rules to protect the natural rights

6 See P.P. Craig, 'Dicey, Unitary Democracy and the *Ultra Vires* Principle', in P.P. Craig, *Administrative Law* (5th edn, London, 2003), pp. 4–7.

7 See Jeffrey Jowell, 'The Rule of Law and its Underlying Values', in Jowell & Oliver, *The Changing Constitution*, pp. 6–16.

of the individual and to discover the means 'necessary to perform the welfare and regulatory functions of modern government' (Jeffrey Jowell). These unpublished lectures tell us more about the separation of powers, the meaning of representative government and the methods and usefulness of amending constitutions so that the government might act justly and function effectively. Dicey touches upon those diverse aspects of constitutional transformation which are both popular and important in the current debate on constitutional democracy in Europe, and particularly in Great Britain: namely, debate on proportional representation and the significance of the referendum, or the badly needed constitutional reform of the House of Lords.[8]

Let us expand a little upon Dicey's opinions. He held that one of the chief characteristics of 'the modern English system' was marked by the existence of a Cabinet system. The Cabinet 'nominally appointed by the Crown' was, in truth, 'indirectly elected by the party which possesses a majority in the House of Commons'. The ruling principle was that 'a Cabinet should retire' whenever the House lost its confidence in the ministers and thus wished their retirement. In any case, a Cabinet was a temporary body, which represented not the nation but a political party, which in turn might fall from power the moment it ceased to be predominant in the House of Commons. This was significant for a constitutional democracy, because the existence of the Executive depended upon the will of the House.

Dicey viewed party government 'as it exists in England' with much scepticism. It demanded 'for its working the existence of two, and not more than two, opposed parties', and the 'essential vice' of party government was that it was 'government by and for a party, and not by and for the nation'. Here most constitutional historians and others advocating reform in the present day would agree with Dicey. He offers suggestions and proposes remedies. Some of these might be introduced without a formal change

8 On this point see illuminating observations by Dawn Oliver in 'The "modernization" of the United Kingdom Parliament', in Jowell & Oliver, *The Changing Constitution*, pp. 161–84.

in the constitutional system, but others need an Act of Parliament. Further, an Act of Parliament – the Constitutional Statute 'itself should not come into force unless within a certain time it was sanctioned by a popular vote and should not be changeable except by an Act itself sanctioned by a popular vote', for the 'sole body which in a modern democratic state' carried 'greater moral weight than Parliament itself is the people, or in other words the majority of the electorate'. Thus Dicey advises us that the system of referendum be adopted, the essence of which 'is that the electors should be called upon to decide sometimes on one of two and sometimes on two points, namely, first, whether there be a constitutional change at all, and, secondly, whether the constitutional change prepared by the legislature is to be accepted'.

In his time Dicey was well aware of the relevance of the voice of the Peers. Any bill affecting the foundations of the Constitution would be automatically rejected by those who regarded themselves as 'guardians' of the Constitution. Therefore no positive gesture from the Lords 'would be really effective without a change in the constitution of the Upper House'. How well Dicey was echoing the sentiments of our own day!

Dicey rightly observes that the English 'Constitution' had grown with the growth of the nation, but then slightly contradicts himself when he on the one hand declares that the 'modern Constitution of England is a *democratic* constitution', and on the other regrets that 'our Constitution knows of no appeal to the people', that it does not make provision for the system of referendum as 'it exists in modern Switzerland'.

Another interesting aspect of Dicey's lectures is that he draws comparison between the British parliamentary government and that of the Swiss, the French and the US. We are given a broader view of the legislative authority of the American Congress and the presidency of the US as well as of the essential features of the French Republican Constitution.

Equally discerning is Dicey's analysis of the Cromwellian Constitution and English Constitutionalism under George III. Dicey examines the Constitution of 1653 not, he says, as a historian but as a legist, and comes to the conclusion that this Constitution was 'an elaborate attempt to create for the Government of England at once a real legislative assembly or Parliament and also a strong extra-parliamentary executive'.

Dicey's interpretations might be open to debate, but it would be rather difficult to challenge some of his assumptions. This is equally true of his analysis of English Constitutionalism under George III. Dicey shows how the Georgian Constitution differed from the constitutional system of his day 'in its form, in its working, in its spirit'. Again, whatever our own views, Dicey's comments are thought-provoking.

The lecture on Party Government is perhaps the most incisive of the lectures delivered by Dicey. The author explains at length the meaning of the Party system, its merits and demerits, the conditions under which it can work for good, the evils which the absence of these conditions produce, and the extent to which the Party system could be dispensed with under a parliamentary constitution. The questions posed by Dicey are not easy, and their solution even less so. And yet what can be said of this lecture, as indeed of all the other lectures printed here for the first time, is that the bright points as well as the dark spots to which Dicey draws our attention in the study of the constitutional systems are highly valuable in guiding us in examining such systems in the present day.

What contribution, we may ask, will the publication of these lectures make to the study of the history of British constitutional thought? We will certainly learn more about Dicey's views on English Constitutionalism than those he expressed in his *Introduction to the Study of the Law of the Constitution*. The study of constitutional thought will be so much the richer as a consequence. We also believe that the exposition of the characteristics of constitutionalism in Britain by Dicey and his comments on Party government will be sure to influence current discussion of constitutional law and offer fresh thoughts to all those (scholars as well as politicians) presently engaged in bringing about fundamental democratic changes in the parliamentary system of our times.

The handwritten drafts of Dicey's lectures were deposited in the Codrington Library at All Souls College, Oxford, sometime in the early

1930s and there they lay. I discovered the Dicey manuscripts (MS 323)[9] only recently. Was it due to accident or luck, or both? Perhaps it was due rather to my persistence in my on-going research. I had been engaged in collecting source material in various archives for a study of the constitutional history of Great Britain, and my curiosity to look deeper into Dicey's works seems to have borne fruit.

While I was examining the Dicey papers I found a covering note by Professor Vernon Bogdanor of Oxford, dated 19 July 1985. He had been invited by the then Librarian of All Souls, Mr P.S. Lewis, to examine the Dicey collection. The material in this collection, writes Professor Bogdanor, 'seems to me of great value to students of constitutional law and constitutional history'. That is how I thought of it myself, and that seems also to be the opinion of Lord Plant of Highfield, Professor of Jurisprudence and Legal Philosophy at King's College, London, who has kindly agreed to write a Foreword to this volume.

I then wrote to ask the Librarian of the Codrington Library, Professor Ian Maclean, for permission to publish the relevant parts of the Dicey

9 This collection contains lectures written in longhand in ink by Dicey on separate sheets. Each lecture has a title; the pages of the sheets of each lecture are numbered, but the sheets are unbound. The lectures consist of an analysis of the English Constitutionalism (which are complete) and an analysis of the constitutions of, chiefly, America, France and Prussia. These lectures are rather scattered. There are also sheets on Scotch, Irish and Australian constitutions. At places sheets are missing especially in the lectures on the constitutions of other countries. In any case Dicey's views of the constitutions of various countries would belong to a separate volume. Putting all these lectures together in one volume under the title, say, of the comparative study of Constitutions would have strongly diminished the significance of the important contribution Dicey has made to the study of the English Constitutionalism. We have thus limited our selection entirely to the lectures on the characteristics of the English system. We might point out here that this selection includes Dicey's extensive references to the distinctive features of the constitutions of other countries. Dicey's handwriting is fine and readable. He might have been preparing the lectures for publication, but it never came to that, perhaps because he seems to have been at this stage more interested in other problems on which he wrote extensively.

collection. The Librarian wrote back that he would need two short letters of support from referees 'who will attest to the value of the project and the suitability of the editor' before permission to publish would be granted. Professor Jonathan W. Wright (Professor of International History in the University of Oxford) and Professor Andrew John Ashworth (Vinerian Professor of English Law in the University of Oxford) graciously supported my request. I am most grateful to both of them. On the basis of this support Professor Maclean wrote to me on 24 October 2007 that he was happy to grant me the necessary permission. I now most humbly acknowledge my gratitude to the Warden and Fellows of All Souls College, Oxford.

At my request a colour transparency of the portrait of A.V. Dicey in Trinity College, Oxford, was kindly loaned to me by the College Archivist Mrs Clare Hopkins to enable me to use the image in my book. For this permission I am grateful to The President and Fellows of Trinity College, Oxford.

I committed myself to work on the present volume during the period of my academic year at Christ Church, Oxford, when I was elected to honorary membership of the High Table and associate membership of the Common Room at this great house of learning for the year 2007/2008. I tender my thanks to the Governing Body for having extended to me this unique distinction, and to Lord Plant of Highfield for his Foreword to the present volume.

Peter Raina
Christ Church,
Oxford
February 2008

Foreword

Lord Plant of Highfield

Dicey's writings on the British Constitution have achieved an almost canonical status. He is still widely cited not much short of a century after his death. Many of the most important books on public law in the UK still devote quite a lot of space to what is usually a detailed critical examination of his understanding of the British constitution, its history, development and implicit principles and the relationship between the constitution and the wider set of political arrangements and indeed to British society as a whole. He was one of a group of nineteenth-century thinkers which also included among the lawyers John Austin and Sir Frederick Pollock whom Stephan Collini has called 'public moralists'.[10] We would now be more likely to call them – following American fashion – 'public intellectuals'. There is nevertheless a significant difference between the two terms. A public moralist for Collini is someone who was integrated into the governing elite of British society and as such their writings on the law, politics and public life generally were accorded greater weight and authority than those whose authors were outside this sort of circle. In our time however, the term 'public intellectual' does not carry that sense of being an insider or part of the establishment. Indeed in our day public intellectuals may be accorded whatever attention they command because, rather than being insiders, they are in fact thorns in the flesh of the establishment. What also helped to establish Dicey as such an important figure has also been well explained by Collini in chapter XI of *That Noble Science of Politics*,[11] namely that at

10 S. Collini, *The Public Moralists* (Oxford, 1993).

11 S. Collini, Winch, D., and Burrow, J., *That Noble Science of Politics: A Study in Nineteenth-Century Intellectual History* (Cambridge, 1983).

the end of the nineteenth century there was a special intimacy in the connection between law and politics which could be taken for granted and that the language of the law constituted a kind of *lingua franca* between history and politics.

Dicey was one of the most eminent public moralists of his time and this was in large part due to the fact that his writings on the British constitution elaborated and defended views about the nature of British politics and law which made much more explicit the ideas which many men of affairs (and they were men) in both politics and law had grasped in more limited and implicit ways. To provide an elaborated account of the inner nature of the British Constitution was no mean feat because the Constitution seems so *ad hoc*, and, if not entirely unwritten nevertheless, as Dicey points out, at least uncodified and unsystematized, and was thought to embody values like freedom, justice and fairness which were left unspecified. An interpretation of this disparate material in a way that was consistent with the history of Britain and one which was sustained for the better part of a century was an achievement of the highest order. There were of course significant critics who were themselves jurists and political scientists of great distinction – Sir Ivor Jennings[12] and Harold Laski[13] for example – but their own critical and even hostile engagement with Dicey is in a sense further testimony to the importance and salience of his views and the same is true today with writers such as Martin Loughlin[14] and Anthony King[15] who have produced books recently on public law and the British Constitution respectively which accord a very important role to Dicey, however critical they are of him.

So what were the salient and central features of Dicey's constitutional understanding? His thought involves a particular focus on the following:

12 Sir I. Jennings, *The Law and the Constitution* (London, 1933).
13 H. Laski, *The Grammar of Politics* (London, 1925).
14 M. Loughlin, *Public Law and Political Theory* (Oxford, 2003).
15 A. King, *The British Constitution* (London, 2008).

the sovereignty of Parliament, the relationship between Parliament and the people, the fact that the Constitution does not differentiate in any way between basic laws with particular constitutional significance and what might be thought of as ordinary law, the role of constitutional conventions, an account of the nature of liberty and rights and a rejection of federalism.

Many of these ideas have formed the stock in trade of constitutional understanding until quite recently. The emphasis on the sovereignty of Parliament, which he defends in the last edition of *An Introduction to the Study of the Law of the Constitution* as still intact despite the passing of the Parliament Act in 1911 restricting the power of the House of Lords, reflects the Hobbesian and Austinian roots of his thought. As a legal positivist he sees the authority of law as lying in its *sources* not in its *content* – moral or otherwise. There are no general principles which underlie law-making, as many common lawyers have thought, but only the will and enactments of the sovereign authority unconstrained by such considerations. If it is its source that makes the law the law, then it is an easy step to take to regard that source as being unitary and sovereign, which is a central theme of Dicey's work. In this approach Dicey was drawing upon the earlier writings of Hobbes (who had argued that there had to be a sovereign law-maker at the basis of each and every legal system),[16] Sir William Blackstone[17] and John Austin.[18] The basic legal source for Dicey is the Crown in Parliament and his understanding of these elements of the Constitution are taken up in the second lecture of the present work. He argues that the legislative authority of the British Parliament is complete and absolute and that no law duly enacted by this body can be regarded as illegal or void even though it might be regarded as immoral, impolitic or unjust. This is a classic statement of the legal positivist position which links the idea of sovereignty

16 T. Hobbes, *Leviathan*, ed. M.J. Oakeshott (Oxford, 1955).

17 W. Blackstone, *Commentaries on the Laws of England Book the First: The Rights of Persons* (Oxford, 1765).

18 J. Austin, *The Province of Jurisprudence Determined*, ed. H.L.A. Hart (London, 1954).

and sources together and rejects the claim that there is any other source of legal authority outside the exercise of sovereignty whether this is to be found allegedly in natural law or in the customs and traditions of the people as exemplified in common law. Dicey was not a believer in what has come to be called the 'common law constitution', that is to say that the common law has some kind of more basic authority than that of the Crown in Parliament. Common law was very important for Dicey but in his view the recognition of its importance did not compromise the sovereignty of Parliament.[19]

So his argument for the sovereignty of Parliament is uncompromising, and it is worth quoting from the lectures:

> the principle then of Parliamentary sovereignty may, looked at from its positive side, be thus described: Any Act of Parliament or any part of an Act of Parliament which makes a new law or repeals or modifies an existing law, will be obeyed by the courts. The same principle looked at from its negative side, may thus be stated: There is no person or body of persons who can, under the English Constitution, make rules which override or derogate from an Act of Parliament or which (to express the same thing in other words) will be enforced by the courts in contravention of an Act of Parliament.

Since law is understood by Dicey to be any rule that will be enforced by the courts, then, as Jeffrey Goldsworthy has correctly pointed out, if the negative criterion is satisfied, then the positive one is too.[20] For Dicey therefore whatever the Crown in Parliament enacts is law, and sovereignty in this unchallengeable form is effectively vested in the majority in the House of Commons.

However, the position is more complex than that, as Dicey recognizes in these lectures. There are two issues here. The first is that he does in fact recognize constraints on the actual exercise of this sovereignty; the second is that if sovereignty effectively resides in the party with the majority in the

19 J. Goldsworthy, *The Sovereignty of Parliament: History and Philosophy* (Oxford, 1999).

20 *Ibid.*

House of Commons then he is interested in looking at how well the party system in fact works in terms of embodying a sense of national will. On the first point Dicey does not, for example, recognize any kind of higher law such as natural law or for that matter the authority of common law if it conflicts with a legislative proposal in Parliament in that if Parliament legislates in a way that compromises common law practices then those have to yield to parliamentary sovereignty. While it may, of course, be unwise for a Government to do this, nevertheless that does not alter the issue of the legality of the legislative act. The real constraint on parliamentary sovereignty is in fact the popular will of the people. The sovereignty of Parliament is limited on every side by the possibility of popular resistance. This is a point taken up in these lectures. Dicey points out that the Constitution is a 'democratic constitution':

> We may call a polity democratic which has two features. The one is that power should finally reside in the numerical majority of the citizens. This is no doubt not as yet in strictness the case in England. One thing is however certain. Every change which has taken place during the last sixty years and every change proposed for adoption is democratic i.e. tends to increase the authority given to the majority of citizens.
>
> The other is the sentiment or conviction which is essentially democratic that the action of the nation in legislation and otherwise ought to be controlled by the will of the majority. This is the substantial meaning of the old phrase the sovereignty of the people.[21]

Dicey seems to be referring to the sheer fact or possibility of resistance as a practical limitation on sovereignty – unlike, for example, Austin who regarded resistance rooted in a sense of positive morality or divine law as legitimate. Dicey is making no such metaphysical claim about the basis of resistance; all he is saying is that Parliament has to take account of the fact that resistance may take place and this is in fact a practical limitation on the sovereignty of Parliament. However, this recognition of resistance

21 A.V. Dicey, *An Introduction to the Study of the Law of the Constitution* (8th edn, republished Indianapolis, 1982).

somewhat differentiates his form of the absolutism of the sovereign from that of Hobbes who regarded resistance as unjustified unless the sovereign threatened a person with death.[22] So, given Dicey's views on this matter, this leads to two questions: how does the sovereignty of Parliament relate to the democratic basis of the Constitution and the sovereignty of the people and how does the action of the majority in the House of Commons in whom sovereignty is effectively vested relate to the will of the people and their sovereignty?

On the first question we might well ask whether we are talking about parliamentary sovereignty or whether we are in fact talking about popular sovereignty. Dicey does indeed recognize the real basis and claim of popular sovereignty, and he gives examples of in the context of the premierships of Lord Palmerston and Mr Gladstone, and he does conclude that 'authorities external to the Houses of Parliament do exercise a certain control over the executive namely the Crown and the country or the electors.' Nevertheless he does argue that there is no way in fact that the people can exert their supreme authority except through parliamentary means. One way of putting the relationship between the sovereignty exercised by Parliament and that of the people is that Parliament is the legal sovereign and the people are the ultimate repository of political sovereignty. This is an important point which, as we shall see in a moment, returns in relation to his arguments about referendums and plebiscites.

If political sovereignty resides in the will of the people we need to consider how far Dicey thinks that the present political arrangements do in fact ensure that the will of the people is known. On this point Dicey has some interesting ideas, which in turn show that he is not in fact a defender of every detail of the British Constitution but is prepared to consider quite radical reforms. There is quite a deep reason for this within Dicey's constitutional understanding and it goes back to remedying some of the defects of party government and the Party system within the House of Commons. As he says in his lectures, the proposals that he is making seem to him to

22 Austin, *op.cit.*

be essential parts of any scheme for diminishing in England the evils of the party system of government. Dicey is very concerned that while it may well be healthy in a parliamentary democracy for parties to clash on issues of principle and to use party discipline in order to pursue these principles, he is concerned that such partisanship may well spill over into the area of the constitution, with constitutional reform or change becoming a strongly partisan issue. So he is interested in ways in which constitutional issues could be taken out of the bear pit of party competition. In this context he writes about strengthening the position of the Crown as a basis for constitutional guarantees but he dismisses that suggestion as unrealistic probably because, as he says in the passage quoted above, the constitution is becoming more and more democratic so the remedy has to be found in democratic rather than monarchical principles. So the two most important issues in this respect to be discussed in these lectures is, first, a reform in the powers and the composition of the House of Lords; secondly he is prepared to countenance a judicious use of referendums. Both of these presuppose reservations on his part that the party system as it operates in the Commons is not working very well as a means of expressing some kind of settled national will and he is interested in proposals that might make Parliament work better.

On the face of it, the House of Lords might appear to be an unlikely candidate if Dicey is searching for mechanisms of greater constitutional protection in a way that is consistent with democracy, but in relation to the House of Lords he argues that it should, indeed could, become the defender of the Constitution by the device of a suspensive veto over legislation which aimed to change constitutional arrangements. The idea here is that the Lords could refuse to pass such legislation until it had been referred to the electorate in a general election, despite the fact that it had been passed by a majority in the Commons. If the ministry which proposed such legislation was returned at the subsequent election and the legislation passed again by a majority (or a 'decided' majority to use Dicey's own term), then it would go through the Lords without further opposition. Although in these lectures he does not elaborate on the point, he does also argue that in order to fulfil this function the Lords would have to be reformed. Presumably his point is that the exercise of a suspensive veto by the Lords in the face of a majority in favour of legislation in the Commons would only be sustainable if the Lords itself had more representative legitimacy Recall that at the time that he was writing the Lords was comprised of hereditary peers, Law Lords (Lords of Appeal in Ordinary) and twenty-six bishops of the Church of England. He does not further speculate on this matter but certainly the basic idea of the second chamber having a suspensive veto has not died away in that it is not unlike a proposal made by the Labour Party at the time of the 1992 general election: the Lords should be made more or wholly democratic but would have a particular role in being able to block constitutional legislation until a subsequent general election.

There is, however, a problem with Dicey's proposal which is in fact a problem from within his own perspective. To put his proposal into practice would be to treat constitutional legislation differently from ordinary legislation, whereas he has argued that all legislation passed by Parliament is on the same level. Constitutional legislation if subject to a suspensive veto by the Lords would then require some kind of cachet attached to it, marking it out as being of this special status. This could be done quite easily by the Speaker of the Commons in the same way that money bills are identified before they come to the Lords as they cannot be blocked by the Lords. However, this would mean that such bills passed by the Commons would be treated differently from other legislation. It is quite a short step from that position to arguing that in fact constitutional legislation should have some more elevated status – that for example it ought to be entrenched in some way or that it cannot/should not be subject to implied repeal. Indeed Dicey recognizes this as a possible consequence of his view and links it to a positive role for referendums.

Dicey is perhaps surprisingly in favour of the sparing use of referendums. This is partly because he is worried about the extent to which the party system as it operates in the Commons might split the political and legal parts of sovereignty – that is to say the sovereignty exercised by the majority in the country and the legal sovereignty vested in a majority in the Commons. As party discipline becomes more and more oppressive – a process which is unlikely to be reversed – then in Dicey's view the legislative outcomes from heavily whipped majorities in the Commons may well drive a wedge between Parliament and the people. In his view the use of referendums could well provide a way of correcting artificial majorities produced by oppressive whipping. This is quite a radical idea from someone who is usually regarded as having a very conservative approach to the Constitution but equally conservatives, not to speak of radicals, have to be concerned about the relationship between popular and parliamentary sovereignty and in Dicey's view the referendum can be a useful tool in this context.

However, in these lectures he spends most of his time discussing referendums in the context of constitutional innovation. He argues that constitutional changes are perhaps the most appropriate subjects for referendums so that they can only be agreed by referendums. This again would require that a proposal should be designated as a constitutional proposal and that breaches the principle that all law is on the same categorical level. A referendum would also in Dicey's view secure special protection for Constitutional Acts, assuming that they had been endorsed in a referendum. This cannot be achieved within Parliament because no Parliament can bind its successor, but nevertheless a compulsory referendum could be a way of giving special status to Constitutional Acts so that a subsequent Parliament might be very wary of repealing any such Act. Indeed, it is part of his view that any such repeal would either be subject to a suspensive veto in the House of Lords or should go to a referendum.

Dicey argues that it would be comparatively easy to mark off certain topics, for example the rights of the Crown, the constitution of Parliament, the Acts of Union and the like, which should be held to be or be made subject of 'fundamental' or constitutional laws and subject to the above processes. In saying this Dicey implies that it would be no great thing to specify certain issues as constitutional, but this can surely be doubted – take for example our contemporary debate on whether or not the Act ratifying the Lisbon Treaty was a way of ratifying a constitutional treaty or not. This question was decided in a very partisan way on all sides in the House of Commons so it seems that there would be a political struggle quite often about which bills did or did not have constitutional salience.

All of this is apart from the issue of how far Dicey's elaborate idea of parliamentary sovereignty and the same status of all law could in fact accommodate the changes which he advocates in these lectures. What does seem to be certain though is that the referendum idea does follow through on Dicey's own insistence that the legal sovereignty of Parliament is actually ultimately heavily constrained by the sovereignty of the people. Indeed, in terms of the proposals that he has mentioned it might be difficult to avoid the view that the legal sovereignty of Parliament is in fact subordinate to the political sovereignty of the people. It is in fact Dicey's strictures on the negative aspects of party government that lead him to the position he holds on both the Lords and the referendum, although it has to be said in the context of these lectures he puts far more weight on the referendum idea than on the Lords. This is interesting in itself because one might have thought that given his high doctrine of the legal sovereignty of Parliament he might in fact have preferred the Lords solution as in a way keeping more of the process of constitutional protection *within* Parliament itself, even though the Lords' power of suspensive veto would ultimately have referred the matter of constitutional change to the electorate in a general election.

There is a further aspect of the referendum proposal in these lectures which is perhaps surprising in that Dicey clearly believes – because he makes the point twice – that referring a constitutional change proposed by the Government to a referendum would still allow that government and prime minister to continue in office even if the referendum were lost. To my mind this is not sustainable. Obviously if the Government took a legislative proposal which fell well short of a parliamentary bill or even Act to the country in a referendum, then it might just be regarded as an issue to which the Government was not wholly committed but on which it sought the guidance of the people – in a sense a referendum on a proposal in a Green Paper. However, even on this basis it seems unrealistic because, if a government thought that a proposal was worth holding a referendum on, then that government, and especially the prime minister, would have to campaign for its acceptance and therefore a defeat in a referendum would be a very considerable blow to a government and the position of the prime minister.

Equally, if this is allied to a point that Dicey does not discuss, namely that it is quite difficult to get people in a referendum to answer only the question asked of them, then often it is clear that a referendum on a particular topic is broadened out into a debate about the whole direction of policy and even the honesty and integrity of the government. Once the debate on a proposal is launched it cannot be kept within narrow parameters, and a defeat in such a referendum would almost certainly be fatal to the government as a whole. It is however rather unlikely that, given the nature of Parliament as Dicey himself describes it, that a referendum would operate in this way because too much of the power of Parliament would be made over to the referendum process with these rather broad and open-ended consequences that I have suggested. It is much more likely that a referendum would be held on a bill which had already passed through Parliament but before receiving royal assent so that Parliament itself had taken advantage of the opportunity to debate and amend any such proposed legislation. Dicey is very vague on this point; he just talks about 'constitutional change prepared by the legislature'. It must be assumed, that Dicey means a full bill because what otherwise does 'prepared by the legislature' mean? Given this understanding then it surely follows that when what must be regarded as a central part of the government's policy was voted down then inevitably it seems to me that the government would have to resign. Dicey is rather panglossian about the possibilities opened up by a referendum in this sort of case because, as he says:

> if it were possible to decide by an honest, popular vote that the great majority of the electors did or did not approve of Home Rule it would be possible without any sacrifice of principle for Lord Salisbury or Mr Gladstone as the case might be, to hold office even though his policy were not adopted.

This seems very fanciful, particularly in relation to the prime minister, perhaps less so in the case of the leader of the Opposition. Given the identification of Gladstone with the proposal, and given the trauma that he had put his own party through to get to the parliamentary stage that he did with the bill it seems incredible to think that he could have survived as prime minister if there had been a negative vote in a referendum. Indeed, this would raise real questions about the accountability of the Executive to the House of Commons in such circumstances.

It is worth pointing out that in the section called '*The rendering the Constitution more or less "rigid" by providing special modes for changing fundamental laws*' (see p. 51), within which the proposals about the Lords and referendums are discussed, Dicey also toys with the idea of a Constitutional Convention as a basic form of protection for constitutional rules. His idea is that such a Convention would be elected *ad hoc* and might consist not of party politicians but rather people with special qualifications in legislation. Given such a composition, such a body might well excel Parliament and, in his words, would carry weight with the public. This Convention could then make constitutional proposals which would certainly have to go to the popular vote but he then goes on to say, 'and (perhaps) ... a Parliamentary vote'. Now this proposal would drive a coach and horses through the doctrine of parliamentary sovereignty if such proposals were to be sanctioned by Parliament. It would do so in at least two ways: first of all this body would have effectively law-making powers if any particular law was endorsed by the electorate and if they were not also subject to a parliamentary vote: note the 'perhaps' in the quotation just given. Secondly, at least for constitutional laws, there would be a body outwith Parliament dedicated to making fundamental laws. It is very difficult to see how this could in any sense be reconciled with even purely legal parliamentary sovereignty, and Dicey does not seriously pursue it much further in the lectures but it does show how radical he is prepared to be and therefore how seriously he takes the issue of the evils of the party system if he is prepared to go to these lengths to contemplate remedies.

He might, of course argue that in fact such a Convention is compatible with parliamentary sovereignty because it would be set up on a statutory basis agreed by Parliament and its existence could be terminated by Parliament repealing that statute. However, the snag with such a view from Dicey's perspective is that he has argued that the proposals that he has made including this one would be ways of protecting constitutional principles but if he is saying that this Convention would be based on ordinary law and could be repealed by ordinary law then the proposals do not seem to have much power in the face of parliamentary sovereignty.

One further point on the sovereignty of Parliament that is worth noting in Dicey's account is in relation to the courts. I shall discuss the more contemporary view of this a little later but Dicey's view is clear and unequivocal, namely that Parliament does not in any meaningful way share sovereignty with the courts. Parliament's legal sovereignty is unitary. The job of the courts is to apply and to interpret where necessary Acts of Parliament. The courts cannot substitute their judgement for that of Parliament or the Executive which is politically accountable to Parliament. The courts cannot invoke ideas of natural law or basic democratic values or the traditional rights and freedoms of common law if these are explicitly abridged, however unwisely, by an Act of Parliament. Professor E.C.S. Wade made this point in his Introduction to the 1964 impression of Dicey's *Introduction to the Study of the Law of the Constitution* when he said that 'No Act of Parliament can be held *ultra vires* on any ground of contravention of generally accepted principles of morality or of law .... No court can declare invalid the provisions of an Act of Parliament on any ground. There is no such thing as the unconstitutionality of legislation by Parliament.'[23] This is an important issue since there has been some suggestion both from judges and academic commentators that in fact at least in the modern context Parliament in some sense shares its sovereignty with the courts – a point to which I shall return later.

23 E.C.S. Wade, 'Introduction' to A.V. Dicey, *An Introduction to the Study of the Law of the Constitution* (London, 1964).

Dicey recognizes that at least parts of the Constitution are unwritten and depend for their effectiveness not on laws and statutes but on *conventions*. He argues that we usually mean three different things when we say that the Constitution is unwritten. The first is that there is no single constitutional document which sets out all the powers and responsibilities of the separate parts of the Constitution: Crown, the Executive, the legislative branch, and the judiciary although, of course, there are documents which have played an important role in the development of the present Constitution. However, he does make an important, and to my mind, very controversial point about this when he argues that the lack of a written constitution is a mere matter of form and that if the main provisions of the Constitution were to be put into a single Act of Parliament then nothing about the Constitution would change so long as that Act could be repealed or amended by some subsequent Parliament. I think that it is difficult to say that things would remain the same because a single Constitutional Act would not just write down the Constitution, but it would also in fact codify it and then when disagreements subsequently arose about its provisions and their correct interpretation then either we would have to rely on conventions to help us through or we would have to empower the courts to rule on disputed powers and disputed interpretations.

The difficulty with using conventions as the way out would seem to lie in the fact that the very pressure to have a written constitution with the effect of codifying it would seem to imply that this would be a response to some problem with the operation of conventions, otherwise why would this process have been undertaken in the first place? I will have more to say about this later. On the other hand, if the courts were to be given this role then it is difficult to see that a written constitution would not have changed the Constitution because it would be difficult to see that Parliament still retained unitary sovereignty if the courts were for example to rule on the proper interpretation of the powers of the Lords and Commons in a Constitution Act when there was a dispute between the Houses about the correct interpretation of the relevant powers. It seems clear that a written constitution implies a codified constitution which in turn is likely to give much more power to the courts to adjudicate on disputes about the meaning of the Constitutional Act. It might of course be possible to think of alternatives which as it were contained such disputes within Parliament. An example might be a forum, say, of privy counsellors drawn from both Houses to deliberate about the respective Houses' powers but if no agreement could be reached then this would still seem to imply that there would be a need for the courts. Indeed, any such forum would be a constitutional addition, particularly if it was set up on a statutory basis.

In Dicey's view there are other ways too in which the Constitution is unwritten are in a sense less problematic, although I shall return later to one of them. The first has to do with the way in which constitutional provisions have emerged from legal decisions rather than from explicit constitutional documents; the second to which I want to return is the fact that the working of the Constitution depends upon conventions rather than on written documents. These conventions are essential to the Constitution but they may well not be written down and they have no statutory basis; nevertheless they do have regulatory effect. As Dicey says, they regulate the public life of England and they constitute part of the 'every civilised polity'. He does make the point that conventions are less important under a written constitution than in the British Constitution just because it is unwritten. However, this rather supports my point made earlier that it is difficult to see from Dicey's perspective why he should have made the claim in these lectures that to move to a written constitution could leave everything as it is (or rather was).

Dicey makes the point in the same lecture that a constitution that is unwritten is likely to be much more flexible and adaptable to changed circumstances than a written constitution. There are several reasons for this important claim. First of all the Constitution Act embodying a written constitution would in practice be much more difficult to change to meet developing circumstances, whereas in an unwritten constitution ordinary legislation can add, subtract or change constitutional provisions in the light of circumstances. So for example the 1911 Parliament Act was an ordinary Act of Parliament but one which drastically modified the powers of the

House of Lords. In an unwritten or largely unwritten constitution there is no categorical difference between legislation. All legislation passed by the sovereign Parliament is on the same level. This was a point which infuriated the Duke of Argyll, a contemporary of Dicey, who in 1888 wrote *The New British Constitution and Its Master Builders* in which he observed of the Constitution that

> Every part of it is at the mercy of ordinary legislation. The process which passes a road act, or delegates to some parochial authority the power of making sewers, is the same process exactly which is competent to subvert the Monarchy, to break up the constitution of Parliament, to confer arbitrary powers upon local majorities ... .[24]

None of it is entrenched, none can bind future Parliaments, or be subject to more complicated processes for amendment or repeal and indeed implied repeal – the basis of a famous case in living memory adjudicated by then Mr Justice Laws when he ruled that the European Communities Act of 1973 could not be subject to implied repeal by weights and measures legislation since it was of such basic constitutional importance.

It is worth pointing out that Dicey's views on the Constitution, and particularly the sovereignty of Parliament, had direct political salience too. It has been pointed out by several commentators that Dicey was quite uncomfortable with the growth of New Liberalism in the 1880s. Indeed this is quite obvious from his 1905 book *Lectures on the Relation between Law and Public Opinion in England during the Nineteenth Century*. This New Liberalism rather eclipsed Classical, Old or Laissez-faire Liberalism and implies a more interventionist state. There were all sorts of reasons for this: social change, the extension of the franchise, the growth of organized labour and philosophical changes too which moved the Liberal Party towards a more social rather than individualistic form of Liberalism. In the

24 George Campbell, 8th Duke of Argyll, *The New British Constitution and Its Master Builders* (Edinburgh 1888), p. 3. Argyll was a minister in Gladstone's first two governments.

intellectual context within which Dicey moved, the work of T.H. Green and other Idealist philosophers had made a big impact, particularly in relation to the idea of freedom. Classical Liberalism had stood for the idea of negative liberty, of freedom as freedom from coercion. What mattered to a liberal society was that individuals were equally free from coercion and equal before the law. On Green's more Hegelian view of freedom as positive freedom, negative liberty was certainly important but so was freedom understood as power and capacity to reach desirable goals. The role of the state was not just to prevent acts of coercion through general laws but to bring resources and opportunities to individuals who would not otherwise be able to act as free agents.[25] As Green pointed out in his lecture 'Liberal Legislation and Freedom of Contract', his view of freedom could be used as a basis for reforming contractual relations and the law relating to them.[26] Dicey regarded all of this with intense suspicion, and in a letter to John St Loe Strachey in 1895 he said of Green's view of freedom that he had given it an 'unnatural and at any rate an unusual meaning'.[27] But semantics was not Dicey's main concern. The central issue for him was that Green's thought had sanctioned an interventionist state or what Dicey called a 'positive state' in the very name of liberalism and freedom. So in his *Lectures on the Relation between Law and Public Opinion in England during the Nineteenth Century*, Dicey says that the fundamental principle of this new political movement was 'faith in the benefits to be described by the mass of the people from the action or intervention of the state'.[28]

So, it might be asked, what has this to do with Dicey's constitutional understanding? The answer is: quite a lot actually because, given his view

25 A. Vincent and R. Plant, *Philosophy, Politics and Citizenship: The Life and Thought of the British Idealists* (Oxford. 1983).

26 T.H. Green, 'Liberal Legislation and Freedom of Contract' (1881), in *Collected Works*, ed. L. Nettleship (London 1885–8), vol. 3.

27 Quoted in W.H. Greenleaf, *The British Political Tradition*, (London, 1983), vol. 2, p. 138.

28 A.V. Dicey, Letter to J. Bryce, 14 August 1898, quoted in Greenleaf, *op. cit.*, vol. 1 (London, 1983), p. 221.

of parliamentary sovereignty in a situation without provision for special protection for basic constitutional forms and articles, such a growth of the interventionist state would actually be easy enough to secure by a party majority in a sovereign Parliament. To put the point another way: there were no constitutional safeguards to secure limited government and prevent the inexorable growth of the interventionist state. Given his view about the sovereignty of the people, and the fact as he noted in the passage cited earlier that the mass of the people will receive benefits from such an interventionist state, then there is the clear basis for the incremental growth of the state underpinned by electoral politics and a Parliament which cannot be constrained in its legislative role. As he said in correspondence with James Bryce, 'the English Constitution is a machine which for good or evil gives effect more immediately than any other polity to the opinion of the governing class, now a wide electorate.'

Although this sort of concern forms a major element in Dicey's *Law and Public Opinion in England during the Nineteenth Century*, it is nevertheless rather inexplicit in these lectures. However, there is one point at which it more or less becomes explicit. He argues that in the eighteenth century the common opinion in Britain, or at least in England, was that the role of the state should be circumscribed and its role was to protect personal safety, freedom and property, but he argues that because of changes in opinion these ideas no longer exert their earlier power. He points out that earlier very little change was effected in the basic functions of the state. However, in the second half of the nineteenth century the growth of the positive state has added new functions to government and this has clearly been facilitated by the sovereignty of Parliament and the lack of constraints on Parliament and part machines within Parliament. He finishes by pointing out his belief that these developments have had a negative effect on freedom and personal independence. Given the way in which he describes the growth of the positive state both in these lectures and in *Law and Public Opinion in England during the Nineteenth Century* it might well seem that he would think that negative freedoms and property rights have constitutional importance because if the Constitution has to do with the basic functions and powers of the state then there is no doubt that these have grown – and in his view to the detriment of negative liberty and the sanctity of private property. So it may well be the case that Dicey's own interest in constitutional safeguards to remedy the defects of the party system have something much more specific underlying them – namely a concern with arresting the inexorable growth of the positive state. This does not undermine the interest or pertinence of his views but it does put them in a perspective as to why a defender of a very orthodox view of the sovereignty of Parliament was so fascinated by constitutional innovations which might be quite difficult to reconcile with the doctrine of parliamentary sovereignty as he taught it.

So, how salient are Dicey's views today? On the one hand there is the view that 'It is hard to question his [Dicey's] doctrine without appearing to lose touch with practical reality. Until very recently, it was almost unthinkable that the courts would ever refuse to apply an Act of Parliament.'[29] There has however been quite a debate by both judges and legal scholars about the continuing relevance of Dicey's basic doctrine of the sovereignty of Parliament. In support of a critical view of Dicey it would be pointed out that many of the basic assumptions which were part of Dicey's settled understanding of the Constitution have now been challenged as the result of constitutional changes over the last generation particularly. Important here are: the passing of the European Communities Act in 1973 and subsequent European legislation and cases decided under such legislation both domestically and by the European Court of Justice; the very considerable constitutional changes introduced by the Labour Government since 1997, including the devolution of powers to a Parliament in Scotland and to Assemblies in Wales and Northern Ireland; the passing of the Human Rights Act to incorporate into UK law most of the provisions of the European Convention on Human Rights; the reform of the House of Lords removing the rights of all but ninety-two hereditary peers to sit and vote in the Lords (with proposed further changes still to come). In addition,

29 T. Allan, *Law, Liberty and Justice* (Oxford, 1993), p. 16.

the draft Constitutional Renewal Bill, which has received pre-legislative scrutiny in Parliament will, if it proceeds to legislation, put the civil service for the first time on a statutory footing and will to a limited degree reform the operation of the royal prerogative and strengthen the role of Parliament in respect of ratifying treaties and in terms of war-making.

At the same time, the growth of judicial review has strengthened the position of the judges, so that some judges are now talking about a kind of dual sovereignty between Parliament and the courts, with governments being politically accountable to Parliament while being legally accountable in the courts. This increased power of the courts has been strengthened by the role of the courts following the passing of the Human Rights Act, which means that they have been given the power to interpret existing legislation so that it becomes compatible with Convention rights as well as the power to declare legislation incompatible with the Human Rights Act while leaving intact the role of Parliament in deciding what to do in the context of such a declaration. The Constitutional Reform Act has also detached the Law Lords from the House of Lords and they will become physically detached in 2009 when they sit for the first time in Middlesex Guildhall as a supreme court, although, crucially, without the power as exemplified in the US Supreme Court to strike down legislation. All of these developments pose powerful challenges to Dicey's understanding of the UK Constitution.

However, it would in my view be a fundamental mistake to regard Dicey's work as irretrievably belonging to the past. This is so for several reasons. First of all and at the most general level of concern, it is still the closest that we have come to a political and legal theory of the disparate and uncodified British Constitution which even after all the changes still remains uncodified and written only in parts. Secondly it is a political theory of the Constitution with which many people agree and they seek to maintain the central insights of that theory.

Take for the moment the central issue of the sovereignty of Parliament. The Government introduced the Human Rights Act but in so doing it went to very great lengths to make the incorporation of Convention Rights into

UK law wholly compatible with a strict interpretation of the sovereignty of Parliament. First of all, incorporation itself was seen as an attempt to bring rights home and to have human rights adjudication done within the British courts according to UK understandings of these rights and their implications. Under the Act judges have an obligation to interpret existing legislation as far as possible to make that legislation compatible with Convention rights, and where a declaration of incompatibility is made it only has an effect if Parliament decides to do something about it by legislating anew or introducing amendments to existing legislation. Even in the Belmarsh case, the judges' judgement did not lead to the release of the prisoners. Rather, Parliament remedied the position by legislating again. So the whole weight of the Human Rights Act has been in fact to emphasize the role of Parliament in maintaining rights by the declaration of compatibility of the face of bills presented to Parliament by the appropriate secretary of state, the role of the Joint Committee on Human Rights which advises both Houses on the human rights implications of legislation and by remedying through legislation or orders incompatibilities when they are declared by the courts. So here has been a major innovation which has been made but in a way that makes it compatible with a wholly Diceyan view of the sovereignty of Parliament.

The same can be argued about parliamentary and ministerial responses to the linked ideas that judges have some kind of theoretical power to disapply legislation if it conflicts with fundamental values – views which have been put forward with varying degrees of forcefulness by Lords Hoffman, Steyn and Woolf and Lord Justice Laws. Lord Woolf, who was at the time Master of the Rolls and Head of the Civil Division of the Courts, argued that there 'are limits on the sovereignty of Parliament which it is the courts' inalienable responsibility to identify and uphold'.[30] Similarly, Lord Justice Laws argued that 'the true sovereignty belongs not to Parliament

30 Lord Woolf of Barnes, 'Droit Public – English Style', *Public Law* (1995), pp. 57–71.

but to the unwritten constitution'.[31] This unwritten constitution involves values such as democracy and freedom of expression, and he went so far as to argue that the judiciary can if necessary invalidate statutes if they conflict with the values of the unwritten constitution. Some elements of the unwritten constitution will be common law principles, while others will be values which are deeply entrenched in the British political tradition – both his examples of democracy and freedom of expression would be examples of those.

Lord Justice Sedley has drawn the conclusion from these and other debates both within the judiciary and in academia that the doctrine of parliamentary sovereignty has to be replaced by what he calls a new and still-emerging constitutional paradigm which is a di-polar or dual form of sovereignty of the Crown in Parliament and the Crown in the courts.[32] The implication of this is that a government is accountable politically to Parliament and legally for its actions to the court. This came to something of a head in the debate over the ouster clause in the Asylum (Treatment of Claimants) Bill. This clause meant that the decision of a tribunal could not be reviewed by a higher court. Many judges expressed deep unease about this clause as conflicting with deep constitutional values and common law principles, and in private some went even further than making unease known. Eventually the clause was dropped, not least because Lord Irvine of Lairg, a defender of a strong doctrine of parliamentary sovereignty and previously Lord Chancellor, made known his own opposition to this clause.

However, as we have seen, in earlier speeches and writings judges had made these claims about their authority and the argument was that they derived this authority either on the basis of basic democratic values embedded in the UK political tradition or from the common law whose values

31 Sir John Laws, 'Law and Democracy', in *Public Law* (1995), pp. 72–93, and also, 'The Constitution, Morals and Rights', in *Public Law* (1996), pp. 622–35.

32 Sir S. Sedley, 'Human Rights: A Twenty-first Century Agenda', in *Public Law* (1995), pp. 386–400, and also 'The Common Law and the Constitution', in Lord Nolan and Sir S. Sedley (eds), *The Making and Remaking of the British Constitution* (London, 1997).

were being threatened, so it was said, by potential Acts of Parliament. Both of these views posed quite a major threat to the Diceyan interpretation of the sovereignty of Parliament and to the view that there could be no authoritative legal sources for the courts to use other than those given by Parliament and the common law where common law provisions had not been displaced by statute. In his riposte to these judicial *obiter dicta* the soon-to-be Lord Chancellor, Lord Irvine of Lairg, in a speech in the Lords in 1996 more or less restated the classic Diceyan account and defence of parliamentary sovereignty. And at the same time, the then Lord Chancellor, Lord Mackay of Clashfern, and the retired Lord of Appeal in Ordinary, Lord Wilberforce, strongly defended the doctrine of parliamentary sovereignty. The view of Lord Irvine was crucial in all of this because as one of those with responsibility for drawing up the Human Rights Act when he came into office in 1997, he produced a framework for the incorporation of Convention rights which made their protection entirely compliant with a Diceyan notion of the sovereignty of Parliament.

The final issue that I want to mention about the contemporary position over parliamentary sovereignty has to do with European Union legislation. The argument is that the European Communities Act of 1973 and subsequent Acts ratifying treaties still exemplify the sovereignty of Parliament since they are still ordinary pieces of legislation which a sovereign Parliament has the power to change or rescind because first of all no one Parliament (that of 1970–4 for example) has the power to bind its successors and secondly because they have no special constitutional protection. The only slight modification to this last claim is that something like the 1973 Act could not be subject to implied repeal by a subsequent Act of Parliament as was established in a judgement by Lord Justice Laws in the Sunderland Market case. As we have seen, Dicey's predominant view was that all legislation is of the same sort, although as we have seen in these lectures he does rather change his mind about this in the light of the growth of the positive state.

Other aspects of constitutional change do not threaten the Diceyan view. The establishment of the Supreme Court has gone ahead on the explicit basis that this court will definitely not have the power to strike down legislation and that its job will be adjudication in terms of statute and common law, as has always been the case, and human rights law which, as I have said, has been made compliant with the doctrine of parliamentary sovereignty. The other big constitutional change has been devolution to Scotland, Wales and Northern Ireland. Now undoubtedly Dicey is a great critic of federalism, and this aspect of his thought is fully reflected in these lectures. No doubt also that some advocates of devolution would see it as a step on the road to a federal UK. However, this is not where we are with the devolution settlement currently in place (supported incidentally in Diceyan fashion as set out in these lectures by referendums in Scotland and Wales and in Northern Ireland). The reason why this is not a federal system is first of all the devolution is rather different in terms of powers in each of the two Nations of Scotland and Wales and the Province of Northern Ireland and different powers are reserved for the Westminster Parliament. Secondly there is no English Parliament and nor is there likely to be and yet this would be a *sine qua non* of a federal system. Finally the legislation makes it clear that this is again ordinary legislation which could be repealed by a future Parliament. Whether it would be wise to do so since the establishment of the devolved bodies was supported in a referendum is another matter, but there is, apart from the *realpolitik* of the referendum results, no entrenched guarantee of these arrangements. The fact is that the referendum does provide a strong political guarantee but not a constitutionally entrenched one. Given this perception we can see that Dicey's ideas about referendums do have substance to them, except for his claim that politicians could stay in office after losing one. What we do lack at the moment is a similar kind of synoptic view as that of Dicey of how the Constitution is developing. What we need, it might be said, is a new Dicey!

However, there might be quite deep reasons why this is not in fact possible. There is a superficial reason which reflects the fact that the Government has gone about constitutional reform in a rather piecemeal and incomplete way – for example with the House of Lords and the powers of a reformed House – a matter of considerable importance to Dicey as we saw. Because reforms have been piecemeal and the process of reform is not yet complete it is rather difficult for any prospective new Dicey to give an overall interpretation of the Constitution as it is now. After all as Hegel said in the Preface to *The Philosophy of Right*, 'The Owl of Minerva spreads its wings only with the gathering of the dusk', and we are not at that stage yet. Equally, the European Union in pursuit of ever closer integration has also engaged in the development of its own institutions which are to a very large degree indeed rooted in the EU Constitution which was aborted by the votes in France and Holland, while the political and constitutional implications of the Treaty of Lisbon have yet to be digested. So there is no doubt that the Constitution is in flux and therefore it is difficult to develop a synoptic view of its present and likely future state.

Nevertheless there is a deeper reason why it is difficult to arrive at such a synoptic view which relates directly back to Dicey and was well put by Nevil Johnson in his important book *In Search of the Constitution*. He points out that for Dicey the Constitution rested on what we might call habits and conventions of behaviour and attitude in politics, the law and indeed in society more generally. These conventions support public morality and, indirectly, public authority. They are part of the way of life of any civilized polity and they are part of the history of constitutional change and development and are part of the genius of a particular people. However, in the modern world these more general conventions and common understandings have been eroded to an uncertain degree. The fact that the constitution once rested upon a level of mutual recognition of convention even when people were strongly divided by party – a point that Dicey makes in these lectures – meant that in Johnson's view there was no real need to refer to constitutional principles and theories. The Constitution in some sense rested on common ethical and political understandings: what, to use Hegel's terminology, might be called 'ethical life' (*Sittlichkeit*). In Johnson's view, however, things have changed fundamentally, requiring a change of orientation in constitutional studies to move towards questions of principle and to address them as such just because they are no longer matters of habit and tradition. What Johnson says here is instructive.

> The contemporary account of the Constitution of this country still owes nearly everything in it to the writers of the last century and notably to A.V. Dicey. For it was he who gave such a large place to convention and attempted to explain how it operated as an indispensable complement to constitutional law proper. But the crucial point is that the power of Victorian constitutional convention is incomparably greater than that of any contemporary convention of the same kind. In saying this I am to some extent doing no more than pointing out how much more seriously our forefathers were committed to the firm observance of a range of moral and political conventions far wider than would be conceivable today. In contrast it is a hallmark of our age that virtually every aspect of social life is caught up in a process of change, is open to challenge, and has lost the kind of predictability which it once had. But for the builders of the Victorian theory of the Constitution there was no need to question the reliance on convention or to believe that they were not building on solid ground. The large place given to convention was precisely the result of a belief that it was founded on habits and traditions expressive of the genius of the people which, like the rock of ages would endure. (It is immensely important to remember how keen a sense of the force of public opinion in society was expressed by Dicey who was a constitutionalist).[33]

This passage has been quoted *in extenso* because it does tell us something very important about why it seems unlikely that we shall be able to have a contemporary Dicey. In Johnson's view, Dicey was able to infuse his constitutional theory with this sense that it did in fact rest upon shared values and a common understanding, a common mind which could and did endure despite party strife and other forms of political controversy. As I have suggested however, Dicey himself saw these understandings as becoming less secure, particularly with the growth of the positive state, and he looked at constitutional innovations as ways of solving these problems. We however live in a rather different world of pluralism and diversity in politics, culture, religion, ethnicity and so forth and those modern

33 N. Johnson, *In Search of the Constitution* (London, 1977), pp. 32–3.

institutions which conservatives of all political persuasions have thought would provide modern ways of forming common values – particularly perhaps public service broadcasting – are all in retreat. So constitutional reform today cannot be guided by drawing out the intimations implicit in common understandings and sentiments since these have been undermined by diversity and moral pluralism. The problem though is that so much of our constitutional understanding is still rooted in these assumptions. Given, for the sake of argument, that we cannot appeal in an uncontroversial way to common understandings we actually have to do something which seems rather countercultural in Britain and that is to appeal to principle and argument in constitutional development and not rely solely on an appeal to common understanding and shared experience.

Peter Raina is to be congratulated for rescuing these lectures from obscurity and securing their publication. The British Constitution is undergoing rapid and profound change and we need to learn from all sources present and past about both the genius of that constitution but also its remedial defects. As these lectures show, despite his innate conservatism Dicey was under no illusions that the Constitution needed to change to meet new circumstances and that creative thinking about new mechanisms was central to this enterprise.

I

Memorandum on English Party System of Government

(6 August 1889)

A. Nature

Under all forms of popular government there must be political parties Englishmen assume that the existence of political parties involves the existence of our system of party government. This assumption is both historically and logically unsound. Our present system is of recent growth & under many forms of popular government it has no existence.

The modern English system is marked by the following characteristics:

1st. The executive is a Cabinet or Committee nominally appointed by the Crown, but in truth indirectly elected by the party which possesses a majority in the House of Commons. By the same party it is kept in power & (indirectly) dismissed.

The indirectness of the method under which a Cabinet is removed from office deserves notice because it has some important practical effects. A Cabinet may indeed be dismissed by a direct vote of want of confidence. In recent times it has more often been displaced by the refusal of the House of Commons to pass some measure or to adopt some policy recommended by the Cabinet. As to the amount of opposition on the part of the House which may justify or necessitate the retirement of a Ministry no definite rule can be given. The ruling principle is that a Cabinet should retire whenever the House shows by its acts that Ministers have lost its confidence, or in other words that the House wishes for their retirement.

2ndly. The members of the Cabinet are, collectively & personally responsible for the conduct of legislation, for the management of the administrative business of the government & for the whole policy of the country both in its general outline & in its details.

3rdly. The Cabinet represents & guides the party, e.g. the Liberals, who have a majority in the House. This party are supposed to possess a coherent body of principles which influence the whole of their policy & which are opposed to the principles of their opponents, i.e. the minority of the House, or in other words the opposition.

4thly. In theory at least the opposition are supposed to be prepared on the Cabinet losing the confidence of the House, to undertake the business of governing the country in accordance with the party principles of the opposition.

5thly. The Cabinet has the power, within certain limits, of dissolving a Parliament from which they do not receive support and of appealing to the country to determine whether the views of the Cabinet, or the views of the House are to be adopted.

6thly. The Cabinet has at its head a Prime Minister, who chooses his colleagues among the principal men of the party to which he belongs and who, if he and a colleague disagree, can require the colleague, if the disagreement be vital, to retire from office.

7thly. The Cabinet is expected to place at the beginning of every session before the country a programme of legislation and more or less takes the credit of the Ministry on carrying this programme into effect.

The general result is that the government of the country is placed in the hands of a committee which represents a predominant party and which is created by & at every moment depends for its existence upon the will of the House of Commons. A Cabinet has neither in theory, nor often in fact, any certainty of existence for a definite period. It is a temporary body which represents not the nation but a party & (subject to the possibility of a dissolution) may at any moment fall from power either by ceasing to command the support of the party, or from the party itself ceasing to be predominant in the House.

Three considerations modify the action of the party system & have hitherto made the Cabinet in reality a more permanent & independent body than might be expected from its characteristics.

The Crown, in the first place, has had, till historically very recent times a considerable part in the appointment of Ministers. They have been more or less "servants of the Crown". Circumstances might even now easily be conceived under which the choice of a Premier, or the exclusion of a particular politician from a Cabinet might depend on the choice of the Crown.

Hitherto, in the second place, an idea has prevailed that at any national crisis, e.g. during a war, a time of disturbance & the like, the leaders of the opposition should support the executive as representing the country, and should, as the expression goes, see that "the Queen's government was carried on".

In the third place the non-Parliamentary members of the civil service are all but irremovable except for misconduct. A permanent Under Secretary of State is supposed never to let his private views interfere with his public duties and may with perfect honour serve every Minister with equal zeal.

These three considerations ought carefully to be weighed. They have hitherto modified in practice the evil results of entrusting the government of a country to a picked body of partisans whose tenure of office depends on their success in guiding their party.

B. Evils

Party government as it exists in England, demands for its working the existence of two, and not more than two, opposed parties.

Even assuming these conditions to exist – and as to this assumption more will be said later – this plan of government has several obvious vices – and vices it must be added not by any means necessarily inherent in the existence of political parties.

1st. Party government through a Cabinet must sacrifice good administration to party exigencies. This occurs in at least two different ways. Leaders are selected for their skill as Parliamentary tacticians & not for their skill as administrators. Half at least of the ablest statesmen are at any given moment excluded from office. No one can honestly doubt that it may well happen that the most competent foreign Minister is a Conservative, the most competent Chancellor of the Exchequer a Liberal, the most competent Lord Chancellor a man who might just as well be termed a Liberal as a Conservative. Yet it is absolutely impossible to bring these three men together into one Cabinet.

2ndly. The essential vice of party government is that it is government by & for a party, and not by and for the nation. And moreover it is a scheme of government under which successful administration or legislation by the executive defers the return of the opposition to power, or to look at the same thing from the other side, under which every failure of the government is *pro tanto*, a gain to their opponents. The inevitable result is that politics becomes a game in a way in which no other serious pursuit of life is turned into a game by men of character. The constant effort of government & opposition must be to trip one another up, or in effect to injure one another at the cost of the nation. Every year there is brought forward bill after bill on the general principles of which men of good sense are pretty well agreed. They could easily be carried were it not that successful legislation strengthens the Cabinet. These are not carried because an

With Compliments

peter.raina@web.de

Magdalen College, Oxford, OX1 4AU

opposition exists to oppose. The same tendency displays itself in matters of administration – even in matters affecting judicial proceedings. Whoever reads the Maamstrasna debates the discussions about Miss Cass,[34] the questions asked, or motions raised about the treatment of political offenders in Ireland, and the like, will see in a moment how the nation suffers because party success depends upon impeding the action of the national government. The harm which is visible is not one half as great as the harm which is unseen. Any knowledge of human nature will convince us that the members of a modern English Cabinet are always trying to avoid offence. Things are left undone which ought to be done, because the doing of them might incur immediate unpopularity. Lincoln[35] saved the U.S. from danger, if not ruin, by surrendering the men taken on board the Trent.[36] Few English Premiers would act as boldly, but Lincoln's tenure of office did not depend on a vote of Congress.

3rdly. Cabinet government of the English type stimulates the demand for constitutional changes while it gives no guarantee that these changes shall be carried out by experts, or be the result of mature deliberation.

This almost of necessity results from the way in which parties bid against one another and from the fact that in England no difference is recognised between fundamental and other laws.

There are very considerable evils in making a Constitution what is called "rigid", but the world has never till recently seen what is likely to be the result of letting the fundamental institutions of a nation be changed at any moment by a party vote. Persons who totally disagree as to the policy

34 [It has been difficult to locate this incident. – Ed.]

35 [Abraham Lincoln (1809–65), president of the US, 1861–5. – Ed.]

36 [In November 1861 the American commander of the Union frigate *San Jacinto* seized from the neutral British ship *Trent* two Confederate commissioners who were seeking the support of England and France for the cause of the Confederacy. The British government sent an ultimatum demanding an American apology and the release of the commissioners. The Trent Affair nearly precipitated war between Great Britain and the US. – Ed.]

or impolicy of Home Rule will yet on reflection admit that such a matter as the Union between England and Ireland, ought not to have been determined by such haphazard legislation as that proposed in 1886. There was a precedent to be found for it in the Tory Reform Bill of 1866,[37] but the precedent was as vicious as the imitation. The vice here signalised is, it may be said, inherent in the English Constitution. The remark is formally true, in substance it is misleading. Till a period of not more than 60 years ago large legislative changes in the Constitution were practically unknown, & even 30 years ago no one dreamt that they could be carried out without lengthy deliberation.

4thly. The party system undermines the belief in the duty due from citizens to the nation. The idea that the state or community has moral rights, to which men of all parties ought to defer, is perishing.

For the spread of this moral disease the party system is responsible. In order that men who in any way respect themselves may act with vigour as partisans, by which I mean as members of a regularly organised body of persons who support the government, or the opposition, as the case may be, it is necessary for them to persuade themselves & others that the differences between themselves and their opponents are vital, and that they differ on fundamental principles. As moreover the weakening of the government is the reason for which an opposition exists, and in England a government can be weakened by attacking both its administration and its legislation – it follows that the opposition for the time being are under the constant & practically irresistible temptation to misrepresent both to themselves and to others every act of the government.

As regards, nine out of ten of the legislative proposals, or the administrative acts of a government there is in England at the present moment, little difference in point either of honesty or of capacity between the conduct of Liberals or Conservatives. On points especially of administration the best

37 [The Reform Bill of 1867 extended the franchise to working classes in towns. – Ed.]

men of both parties are substantially agreed. Such men when in office to whatever party they belong, transact the business of the country to the best of their ability, and whatever their good intentions or capacity, never avoid a large number of blunders. Yet each party when in opposition, attack the conduct of the government both as a whole and in details. Men actually engaged in politics soon come to believe that their opponents cannot do right on any point whatever. Hence further the Government of the day is considered not as the government of the Crown or of the country but as the government of a faction & what the government is considered to be, that it is likely in fact to become. This tendency to look upon the government as in some way opposed to the nation of which it is really the organ is in England stimulated by historical causes. Modes of thought & feeling appropriate to the time when the country was really engaged in a contest with the Crown have survived to a period when the authority of the Crown is only a name for the authority of the State.

5thly. The party system may well have the effect that half the policy pursued by the Cabinet is not the policy approved by the nation. The majority of the electors wish say to maintain the Union & for a pacific foreign policy. The Conservative leaders advocate the maintenance of the Union and a warlike foreign policy, the Liberals a peaceful policy abroad & Home Rule in Ireland. Neither party when in power carries out the will of the nation.

6thly. The party system, if it is to work even tolerably depends upon the existence of conditions which can as a matter of fact be found only under exceptional circumstances.

These conditions are the existence of two parties, and of no more, each of which is held together by belief in a more or less complete and coherent political creed and each of which disbelieves in the creed of its opponents.

In a very rough way this state of affairs has existed in England, and in some other countries as long as there was a bona fide contest between the advocates & opponents of democratic government. But the establishment of popular government has in England at any rate, obliterated this broad line of division between two leading parties. This want of a real division which has been often felt in other countries as well as in England has two effects. It induces political leaders to find out or invent causes of division. In other words it gives a factitious stimulus to agitation; it further is favourable to the rise of groups or factions. These may be bodies which are united by belief in the supreme importance of some particular principle or measure. Such are the anti-vaccinationists, the temperance party, the Irish Home Rulers. These groups again may be real factions, that is knots of men allied together for the sake of promoting the political interests of themselves or their followers. The appearance of these groups or factions is fatal to the existence of a strong government and a strong opposition. In France where this modern Parliamentary disease shows itself in its worst form any Ministry can be turned out by a temporary coalition of factions. But the groups which have for the moment coalesced are unable to lay the foundation of a strong government. The national executive is placed at the mercy of intriguers. This malady of modern Parliaments prevails be it noted in every part of the civilized world. In France, in England, in the U. States, in Switzerland, men suffer from the evils of "Parliamentarism" though it is only in one or two of these countries that the infliction has as yet obtained a name.[38] It is only however where the Cabinet system of party government prevails that Parliamentarism can, as in France, reach its full development. Where the executive does not depend from day to day for its existence on the vote of the legislature, the divisions of the legislative body need not necessarily weaken the executive.

38 See especially Bryce's account of American State Legislatures [in James Bryce, *The American Commonwealth* (3rd edn, London, 1893). – Ed.]

C. Mitigations or Remedies

The object of all the mitigations or remedies proposed for the lessening or the removal of the bad results of the party system is in the main to restore the nation to control over its own destinies by placing the national executive and the fundamental institutions of the State so far at any rate out of the reach of party that the one cannot be overthrown & the other cannot be suddenly changed by the sudden whim either of the House of Commons or of the electors whom the House of Commons represents. Under a system of popular government, such as does exist & practically must exist in England it is vain to suppose that any constitutional devices can make it impossible for the nation, that is for the distinct majority of the electors to get rid of any government or institution, which the nation deliberately condemns. What, if any, may be the means of checking the progress of democracy, or what, if any, the methods of overthrowing a democratic form of government are questions with which this memorandum has no concern whatever. They are enquiries, it may be added, with which no sensible Englishman will at the present day trouble his head. What this memorandum is concerned with is how far in a democratic State, like modern England, it is possible to get rid of the modern system of party government or to mitigate the evils which it entails. That such removal or mitigation is possible is proved by the experience of other countries, notably of the U.S. (of Germany?) and of Switzerland.

I. Remedies which might be introduced without a formal change in the Constitution

i. The authority of the Crown as standing outside & above the conflicts of party might be considerably increased & this without any change in the form of the Constitution.

There are one or two administrative functions which even now were better left in the hands of the Crown than of the Ministry. Such are the "pardon" [*sic*], in the strict sense of the term, of offences; the appointment of military or naval commanders, and (under conceivable circumstances) the conduct of foreign affairs (?) [*sic*]. Of course by "pardon" I do not mean the reinvestigation of a prisoner's guilt; what is meant is the determination whether under certain circumstances, the legal guilt being established, punishment is to take effect. I doubt whether any modern Ministry would venture to hang a clergyman as popular as Dodd.[39]

Suppose, for example, (and the supposition is not in itself by any means inconceivable) that the mass of the electors were to feel that a King more nearly represented their general & permanent wishes than did a Cabinet or a Premier appointed by a fluctuating party, & were therefore to allow the King considerably more authority than the Queen now exercises in determining the Constitution and the conduct of the Cabinet. Such a state of feeling would, it is clear, modify the whole working of the Constitution. There are many circumstances, not necessary here to work out, which suggest that a democracy might be far more willing than were the aristocracy of the last century to constitute the Crown a kind of arbitrator among parties. The constitution of the French Republic embodies an attempt though not a very successful one to create a head of the executive who without coming

39 [William Dodd (1729–77), Church of England clergyman, convicted of forgery and hanged 27 June 1777; see J. Villete, *The Trial of the Reverend Doctor William Dodd* (1777). – Ed.]

into conflict with the Parliament, should stand above the Ministry of the day. Nor is there any reason in the nature of things why a King who shared popular sentiments or prejudices should not, like George III in the later part of his reign, represent the national will more truly than any Minister. Even as it is a King could at present probably exert on one or two matters, a kind of influence upon opinion, to which for sixty years Englishmen have been quite unaccustomed. It is further possible though far less probable that the miscalled "veto" [*sic*] might be revived in regard to great constitutional changes, as a "suspensive veto" which could be used in place of the "final veto", which is unusable. Any plan however for increasing the influence of the Crown is at the present moment not worth discussion. It depends upon having on the throne a King of at any rate more than average capacity who should have gradually acquired as did George III weight & authority among the mass of the people.

ii. The House of Lords might constitute itself the guardian of the Constitution.

Taking warning by the fate of the Royal veto the House might while there is still time transform its nominal power of finally rejecting bills into a real & valuable suspensive veto on constitutional innovations.

To achieve this end no formal changes in the Constitution is absolutely necessary. It would be attained if the leader of the majority among the Peers announced, with the consent of followers who were prepared to act on the announcement, that henceforth any bill affecting the foundations of the constitution from whatever side it proceeded would be rejected by the House in order that its provisions might be submitted to the electors on a dissolution of Parliament and that any bill would after being so submitted & having again passed by a decided majority through the House of Commons, be passed by the Peers.

The announcement may appear vague; almost all constitutional understandings are in their nature vague. They are not the less easy to act upon by politicians who honestly mean to give effect to them.

Such an announcement as has been suggested would (little as M.P.s believe this) give no offence to the electors, whose authority it would distinctly acknowledge & increase. It would raise the power of the Lords, for a rejection of a bill would thenceforth cease to mean a threat of thwarting the popular will. As things now stand a rejection of a measure involving large changes has in reality pretty much the effect that the proposed announcement ascribes to it. But the formal surrender of a right of final veto which cannot be exercised would take away all offence from the actual exercise of a suspensive veto, which entails nothing but a referendum to the people. The House of Commons would be the loser, but to anyone who wishes to reform the present party system the House of Commons is the enemy.

No changed action however on the part of the Lords would be really effective without a change in the constitution of the Upper House.

iii. The older practice might be revived of a Ministry retiring only after a formal vote of want of confidence by the House of Commons.

It lies in the hands of any government to proclaim its resolution to take this course. The change may seem a small one, but it would give a not inconsiderable check to attacks on measures which are assailed not because really objected to in themselves, but because the rejection of any measure always damages and often may turn out a government. It lies rather beyond the scope of this paper to consider the various methods by which the "debating", so called of the House of Commons may be cut short. The waste of time in a debate on the address be curtailed, frivolous questions be put an end to, and the like. It will some day be worth consideration whether an annual Queen's speech is of any good whatever; the harm it works is much more clearly manifest than the benefit. These details are mentioned here only because to diminish the possibilities of Parliamentary obstruction is indirectly to check the development of the party system.

iv. By a change in constitutional understandings, which is also something like a return to an older system, certain members of the Cabinet might be treated as in the main departmental Ministers, and not be expected as an invariable rule to retire with their colleagues.

Such for example might be the Chancellor, the Minister of Foreign Affairs, the Secretary at War, & the First Lord of the Admiralty. Of course there are many cases in which one or all of these Ministers might fairly be expected to retire, but there is in the nature of things no reason why a Lord Chancellor, or a head of the Admiralty should have any special views upon say Home Rule or the right policy to be pursued in Afghanistan. And the foreign policy of the country ought as a general rule to be so continuous & so clearly based upon plain facts which statesmen of opposite sides may recognise, that the same foreign Minister might, one would suppose, pursue his proper work in spite of a change of colleagues, caused say by the rejection of a bill for the reform of the poor law. Of course such an arrangement would involve the result that these permanent Ministers would take comparatively little part in the general policy of the Cabinet. It would be curious to ascertain what part they even now take as a rule in matters not concerning their own department. It would however be compatible with the rule that any of these departmental Ministers should retire whenever the Cabinet was defeated on a subject concerning the department of such Minister, or whenever his views as to the conduct of his department disagreed with the views of the Cabinet. Even in France where Parliamentary control has been fatal to the stability of Ministers the advantage of a continuous foreign policy has led to an effort to keep foreign affairs in the hands of a Minister not changing with successive Cabinets. Were it not for the influence of party customs it is difficult to see why for example

Lord Roseberry[40] or Lord Herschell[41] should be incapable of discharging their appropriate duties in Lord Salisbury's Cabinet[42] simply because they disagree with the Premier on the matter of Home Rule. One advantage of retaining departmental Ministers in office would be that statesmen who are eminent specialists in particular lines would not be called upon either to form or express decided opinions upon questions as to which they speak with no special authority whatever. The existence however of departmental Ministers depends upon, or is closely connected with the possibility of giving "rigidity" to the constitution & thus restricting the sphere of Parliamentary legislation.

II. Remedies which involve a formal change in the Constitution

i. The introduction of some form of Presidential government, combined as it almost inevitably would be, with the establishment of a written Constitution containing fundamental laws.

This "Americanising" of the English Constitution would not of necessity be incompatible with the formal maintenance of the Crown. There might indeed be some gain in separating the ornamental part of the Constitution from the office of elective Prime Minister or President. Still the plain truth is that things being as they are the nominal authority of the Crown makes it extremely difficult to establish a really fixed executive, not depending

40 [Lord Archibald Rosebery (1847–1929), prime minister, 1894–5. – Ed.]

41 [Lord Farrer Herschell (1837–99), liberal politician, lord chancellor, 1886, 1892–5. – Ed.]

42 [Lord Robert Salisbury (1830–1903), prime minister, 1885, 1886–92, 1895–1900, 1900–2. – Ed.]

on the vote of the House of Commons. Moreover it is all but inconceivable that such a change as that suggested could be brought about without a revolution.

ii. The appointment by Parliament of a Cabinet which shall hold office for a definite period, namely until the convocation of a new Parliament.

This innovation may it is likely enough be in fact though not in theory introduced without any legal change in the Constitution. The experience of the last 20 years suggests that a Ministry gains nothing by a dissolution. If this be the fact a Cabinet once secure of a Parliamentary majority will as a rule continue in office for at least the length of each Parliament.

If however the fixity of the executive is to be secured, changes both of law and of custom are requisite. Probably the duration of each Parliament ought to be fixed so that irregular dissolutions should be altogether avoided. This in its turn would it may be suspected necessitate the shortening of the period for which each Parliament should exist to a time say of three or four years.

This alteration in the tenure of office is almost inevitably connected with other alterations in the Constitution, such as the introduction of the distinction between "constitutional articles" and ordinary laws.

iii. The rendering the Constitution more or less "rigid" by providing special modes for changing fundamental laws.

It would be comparatively easy to mark off certain topics, e.g. the rights of the Crown, the constitution of Parliament, the Acts of Union, and the like, which should be held to be, or be made the subject of "fundamental" or "constitutional laws", & to provide that these articles of the Constitution should be altered by Parliament only in a special manner, e.g. by a two thirds majority of both Houses, or after the proposal to alter any of these articles had been made in one session and adopted in another.

Nor is it certain that such a provision might not have a considerable practical effect in ensuring deliberate procedure in the making of constitutional changes. Still it is more likely than not that the effect of these provisions would be small & that they would fail just at the times when it was most desirable that they should have effect, i.e. at periods of momentary popular excitement. Artificial devices, of the kind suggested, encourage violent methods of forcing through changes approved by public opinion, and what in England is of more consequence, foster political intrigue, & even corruption.

The only means (as far as experience guides us) for placing the foundations of the Constitution beyond the reach of the ordinary legislation or Parliament, is to provide for their change by some body which may carry greater moral weight than Parliament itself & whose commands may be treated by the Courts as superior to the commands of Parliament, i.e. to an ordinary statute.

The sole body which in a modern democratic state, such as England, which carries greater moral weight than Parliament itself is the people, or in other words the majority of the electorate.

It is idle for the present purpose to discuss whether the deliberate voice of the majority ought to command this moral weight. All that is necessary for the present purpose, is that in a modern democratic state the will of the electors is finally and in the long run decisive, and that there is no other power of which the influence can as things now stand conceivably overbalance that of Parliament.

If therefore it be desirable to place certain fundamental articles on a different basis from that of ordinary acts, this can be achieved only by in some form or other obtaining for these fundamental articles a popular sanction not directly given to other laws.

Let me to illustrate & explain my meaning, assume that it is thought desirable to make the Acts of Union, either as they at present stand, or after being remodelled, fundamental articles of the Constitution.

The following is the sort of method to be pursued.

An Act of Parliament – the Constitutional Statute – should be passed enacting that the Acts of Union should not be changed except in the manner therein provided which manner should provide in some shape or other for submission of the change to a popular vote.

The Constitutional Statute should also enact that the Constitutional Statute itself should not come into force unless within a certain time it was sanctioned by a popular vote & should not be changeable except by an Act itself sanctioned by a popular vote and that any Act of Parliament or portion of an Act either directly or indirectly contravening the Constitutional Statute should be, and should be held by the Courts to be, void.

The possible methods for submission of the Constitutional Statute or of changes therein to a popular vote are speaking roughly, twofold.

First. The constitutional convention, such as prevails in the United States, & such as in effect though not in name, drafted the Canadian Constitution.

Such a convention being elected *ad hoc* and consisting as it ought to do, and might of persons who have special qualifications as legislators and are not ordinary party politicians is likely both to excel Parliament in legislative skill and to carry weight with the public. In order moreover to give additional force to the resolutions of the convention they should before they became laws obtain the sanction of a direct popular vote and (perhaps) of a Parliamentary vote (which should be confined to passing or rejecting the Bill as it came from the Convention).

Secondly. The Referendum, such in substance though not of course in details, as it exists in Switzerland.

The essence of this system is that the electors should be called upon to decide sometimes on one of two & sometimes on two points, namely, first, whether there be a constitutional change at all, &, secondly, whether the constitutional change prepared by the legislature is to be accepted.

If the system of the Referendum were adopted (which it is apparent is combinable and in America is in reality combined with that of the Convention) then the Constitutional Statute could never be changed unless the change were approved after deliberation by the majority of the electors.

All this constitutional machinery, it may be objected, would be futile because Parliament might of its own authority by a subsequent Act alter or repeal the Constitutional Statute.

The objection is plausible, but at bottom futile. It implies that a sovereign power can never surrender its sovereignty which really amounts to saying that the acts of men can be tied by the forms of logic and in this case by a misapplication of such forms. The plausibility of the objection arises from the known fact that Parliament has altered the apparently unalterable provisions of the Acts of Union. The essential difference between these Acts and the supposed Constitutional Statute is that they did not receive, and the Statute would receive a sanction beyond that of Parliament. The Acts of Union moreover instituted no other body than the United Parliament, capable of changing them. It therefore became absolutely necessary that the United Parliament should exercise or assume the power of amendment or repeal.

Grant however, for the sake of argument, that the Imperial Parliament *could* by a subsequent Act repeal the Constitutional Statute. There is no reason to suppose that in fact Parliament would do so. Such a repeal would be a direct defiance of the real sovereign authority, namely a majority of the electors, and would therefore hardly be attempted by men who certainly do not err by want of deference to electoral opinion.

Of the two methods by far the best from a jurisprudential point of view is that of the "Constitutional Convention". The alteration of the Constitution by a body elected *ad hoc* and which undertakes no other business than that of preparing a special scheme of legislation, is in itself a great improvement on what may be called the Parliamentary or "constituent" method of constitution making. It happily separates legislation on most important points from the question what men and what party are to remain at the head of the administration.

The Referendum is on the other hand by far the most easy method to pursue. It might even, as already pointed out, be indirectly imported into the Constitution without the necessity for legislative change by the mere action of the House of Lords. This perhaps is a convenient opportunity for adding that for the proper carrying out of any change which shall correct the evils of the party system, the reform of the House of Lords is all but essential. It is now for all practical purposes a party body. In order that it may represent national Conservatism it must cease to be an instrument of the Conservative party. It should be greatly lessened in numbers, it should become in great part at least, representative; it should admit all Ministers to its debates, & if possible, force on the House of Commons the admission of all Ministers to debates in that House. The one policy of the House should be to become the guardian of the Constitution by representing the permanent wish of the nation against the factitious combination of Parliamentary groups or factions.

To the Constitutional Convention, & still more to the Referendum, it is objected, and with truth, that they each tend to decrease the importance of the House of Commons & of Parliamentary debate. This is undoubtedly their bad side. They are however either alone or in combination, essential parts of any scheme for diminishing in England the evils of the party system of government. Take however the Referendum which is the most open to theoretical objection, and consider the great advantages which might counterbalance its admitted evils.

1st. The very charge, though not I think fully made out, that the Referendum impedes salutary reforms is only another way of admitting that it prevents legislation which goes much beyond popular opinion. This in some cases is a great advantage. It would have been a great gain could the policy of the Contagious Diss. Acts[43] have been originally submitted to a popular vote. If the policy had been approved a reform would have been secured. If the policy had been disapproved a futile attempt at reform would have been avoided as well as disgraceful concession to a very damaging agitation.

2ndly. The Referendum brings clearly before the nation that the law is the decree of the people for which they are responsible and not a rule made by the oppressors of the people which lawbreakers can defy in the name of the people.

3rdly. The Referendum makes it possible for statesmen honourably & honestly to conduct the affairs of the country even though on some points the policy of the nation does not agree with the views held by some of the executive.

Thus if it were possible to decide by an honest, popular vote that the great majority of the electors did or did not approve of Home Rule it would be possible without any sacrifice of principle for Lord Salisbury or Mr Gladstone[44] as the case might be, to hold office even though his policy were not adopted. There is nothing disgraceful in carrying out to the best of one's ability the business of an employer who in some respects pursues a course of which his possibly better instructed agent does not approve. What is disgraceful is for the agent to surrender his own opinion or to pretend that he agrees with his employer. The truth is that the Referendum would lead quickly to that kind of decision which even now when it is obtained after years of party contest every sensible man admits

43 [Clergy of the Church of England desired the Contagious Diseases Acts to be repealed, 1883, 1884; see *Parliamentary Acts, Vict.* 1884. See also Sir James Stansfeld, *On the Failure of the Contagious Diseases Acts, as proved by the official evidence submitted to the select committee of the House of Commons, 1879, 1880 and 1881* (London, 1881). – Ed.]

44 [William Gladstone (1809–98), prime minister, 1868–74, 1880–5, 1886, 1892–4. – Ed.]

to be final. No one ever blamed Peel[45] for accepting the Reform Act after opposing the Reform Bill.

4thly. The Referendum separates in the mind of the people the question of measures from the question of men. It prevents the inextricable confusion between the effect of a proposed law and the effect of keeping certain persons in power. At this moment half the Home Rule electors would it may be suspected give up Home Rule if without Home Rule they could have Gladstone as Premier.

Thus the Referendum cuts at the very root of the English party system and when difference of opinion is not needed to support distinctions of party differences of opinion become far less common & far less important. It is moreover quite one thing to say that the mass of the electors are incompetent to pronounce on legal details & quite another to assert that they are incompetent to pronounce on general lines of policy. Their real or supposed competence in this respect is the essential basis of modern popular government & what can be said against the Referendum may be urged in the main against democracy itself.

I am quite aware however of the evils actual & possible of this institution. All I urge is that in some modified form it may be used as a corrective to the English party system.

N.B. To the Referendum is, I suspect, due the stability of the Swiss Council or Cabinet. Its members though elected every 3 (or 4 ?) [*sic*] years, are constantly re-elected. It is, as every Executive ought to be a permanent body of trained officials. Contrast this with the Ministeries of England, France, or Italy, and even with the Presidential government of America. The contrast with France is particularly instructive, because, if it be objected, as with some plausibility it may, that the stability of Swiss administration arises from one party (the Liberals) having been permanently in power, it

45 [Sir Robert Peel (1788–1850), prime minister, 1834, 1841–6. – Ed.]

should be observed that in France also one party, namely, the Republicans have been in power since the fall of MacMahon.[46]

It may further be noted that the suggestion that Ministers may under the Referendum creditably carry on the administration even though the people refuse to sanction some part of the ministerial policy is no more than suggesting that the heads of the Executive may in the case supposed, occupy a position similar to that filled with the highest honour by all permanent civil servants in England.

46 [Marshal MacMahon was second president of the Third Republic (1873–79); see further Alfred Cobban, *A History of Modern France* (London 1963), vol. II, pp. 199–200. – Ed.]

2

General Characteristics of Existing English Constitutionalism

(5 May 1897)

Let us look at the existing Constitution from two or three different points of view.

A. The modern Constitution of England is an *historical* Constitution

This is a statement which we all of us constantly make in one form or another & no one is the least tempted to deny, but of which it is more difficult than at first sight appears to appreciate the full meaning. In one sense every human institution & therefore every polity is historical. It has come into existence through a definite set of events. It connects in some way or other with the past. Thus to take the French Republic which has existed for not more than a quarter of a century. It certainly is the product of history. The story of its formation is a very curious one. A student can hardly understand a line of the constitutional laws unless he bears in mind the events of 1870 & of the years which follow. The fall of the second Empire, the German invasion of France, the Conservatism of the Assembly at Versailles, the insurrection of the Commune, & many other well known events must be borne in mind if we are to explain either the proclamation of the third Republic or the peculiar & fragmentary form of the laws governing the French Commonwealth. Nor again can the working of French institutions be understood unless we go a good way back into the history of France. Unless we take into account both the causes & the results of the great Revolution. Thus, to give one example, the power & the incapacities of the French magistracy or as Americans would say of the Judiciary are demonstrably the result, though it may be the result by way of reaction, of the condition of the French *Parlements*. The French Constitution therefore is in one sense historical, but every one feels that it is not an historical constitution exactly in the sense or more strictly in the senses in which we apply the term to the English Constitution & the same remark applies to the Constitution say of Italy, of Belgium, of the German Empire, & indeed of almost any European State with the possible exception of Hungary.

If then every Constitution has a history & has links with the past what do we mean when we apply the term historical to English institutions as marking off a difference between them & the political arrangements of other lands.

The statement that our Constitution is an historical Constitution includes at least three ideas which though often blended or confused together, are distinguishable.

1. The English Constitution has been *historically* developed. It has grown, that is to say, with the growth of the nation. The Crown, the Parliament, the Courts, the national Church, as they now exist are each of them the gradual creation of the course of events which make up the history of England. Thus it is absolutely impossible to explain either the constitution of the existing Parliament, or the position of the Church of England, without constant references to past history. No doubt in one sense this, as I have said, is true of all institutions at all times & every where, but it is not true of all institutions in the same sense. It is quite possible to state for example, the Constitution of the French Senate & to enumerate the powers of that body without going further back than the date at which the Senate was created. There is no need for tracing its descent from any

prior assembly, as for example from the order of the noblesse in a States Generale from the Senate of Napoleon I, from the House of Peers under the Bourbons or the Orleanist dynasty, or from the Senate of the second Empire. I have said there is no need to trace this descent – I ought rather to have said there is no possibility of doing so. You cannot explore a genealogy where no genealogy exists. This difference between the House of Lords & the French Senate forms a distinction between the whole of the French & the whole of the English Constitution. The one has not & the other has been the result of historical development.

2. The Constitution has been *continuously* developed. There has been no break in the growth of the English Parliamentary system.

The Parliament of today differs in material points from the Parliament of say Henry VIII just as the Parliament of Henry VIII differed from the Parliament of Edward I, or the Parliament of Edward differed essentially from the Magnum Concilium of the first Norman Kings & the great Council in its turn differed greatly from the Witenagemot[47], but each of the stages of Parliamentary growth are linked together you may say that the Parliament of one age is the same Parliament as the Parliament of the next something in the same sense in which you may say that a man of 70 is the same person as the boy of 7 years old. You may of course point out eras at which the fabric of the English Constitution has undergone changes or developments, such for example is the Revolution of 1688, the date of the Union with Scotland 1706,[48] or the date of the Union with Ireland 1800, or the crisis which ended in the passing of the Reform Bill of 1832.[49] But

47 [Earliest national parliament; see further Ann Lyon, *Constitutional History of the United Kingdom* (London, 2003), pp. 5–6. – Ed.]

48 [See 'Act for the Union with Scotland, 1706', in W.C. Costin & J. Steven Watson, *The Law and Working of the Constitution. Documents 1660–1914* (London, 1953) *Vol. I, 1660–1783*, pp. 98–111. – Ed.]

49 [Reform Bill of 1832 'largely destroyed the control over Parliament which the Crown had for more than a century possessed through the use it made of influence and patronage. It gradually became plain that the Reform, if in many ways limited and conservative, had had at least two really revolutionary effects. The first was that the

though you may point to changes, & great changes you cannot point to any distinct break, with one possible exception, in the development of the Constitution. Continuity it is true is not identity, but practically unbroken continuity is undoubtedly one of the features in the development of English institutions which makes them emphatically historical.

Contrast this unbroken growth of the English Parliamentary system with the history of the modern German Empire or the modern Swiss Confederation. Both of them are in a very true sense historical Constitutions. They are connected with the past history of Germany or of Switzerland respectively in a way in which the French Republic is not connected with the past history of France. They give effect to ideas which have been working with more or less distinctness for centuries amongst the German & the Swiss people. The German Empire could not be what it is were it not for traditions & sentiments dating back to the Holy Roman Empire. It would be absolutely impossible to understand many of the anomalies in the Imperial Federation, e.g. the constitution & position of the Bundesrat, unless you took into account the state of things which existed under the Empire up to 1800 & further under the Confederation from 1815 to 1866. The Empire dates from 1871 but it is the result of tendencies which have been working for centuries. From one point of view it is the restoration or revival of an older state of things. The modern Swiss Republic dates indeed from 1848, but it is distinctly the result of that constant effort towards national unity which amidst all the struggles & confusions which perplex any man who

King could no longer choose his ministers at his sole discretion and furnish them, so long as they retained his confidence, with a parliamentary majority generally reliable under normal conditions. The second was that the Lords, hitherto so closely linked with the Commons that constitutional conflicts between the Houses were of rare occurrence, had lost their former position, that the ascendency had now passed to the Lower House, which found in its own popularly-elective character a basis for resisting the claims of a non-elective assembly to act as an independent and even rival force. The collective effect of these two changes was momentous'; see Sir David Lindsay Keir, *The Constitutional History of Modern Britain, 1485–1951* (5th edn, London, 1953), pp. 373–4. – Ed.]

studies the annals of Switzerland is the true note or mark of Swiss progress. Yet though the modern German Empire & the modern Swiss Republic are in one sense historical constitutions they each lack the characteristic of continuity. It is indeed quite conceivable that under different circumstances the German Imperial Constitution of today might have stood in unbroken connection with the Holy Roman Empire. It is even more easily conceivable that a process of gradual reform might without any break have transformed the Swiss Confederacy as it existed in 1789 into something like the modern Swiss Republic. But as a fact this gradual development did not take place. In each case the French Revolution broke the line of historical continuity. The Holy Roman Empire ceased for a time to exist. The institutions by which it was replaced were not linked to it. Take the example of Switzerland which is a very striking one. You can say with truth that the habits & sentiments created by the old confederacy gave birth to the modern Confederation, but it is impossible to deny that the French Republic & the Napoleonic Empire interrupted the course of Swiss constitutional development. The unitary Helvetic Republic modelled under the influence of French politicians & reproducing the ideas & institutions which prevailed in France in 1797 stands apparently at least unconnected with the Confederacy of the Thirteen Cantons & unacknowledged by the modern Republicanism of Switzerland. It occupies a position not absolutely unlike the position occupied by the Commonwealth of the Protectorate in the history of England. It is worth turning for a moment to the Commonwealth. It illustrates by way of contrast the matter under consideration. Had the Constitution of 1653 created by the Instrument of Government held its ground the country might have gained many & considerable advantages. But English constitutionalism would have lost its specially historical character. The political institutions of the country would have dated back to a definite year, & there would have been a distinct breach in their continuity. The artifices of lawyers can achieve much but it would have taxed & overtaxed their astuteness to show that the Parliament created by Cromwell[50] & his officers with its single House & with its representation of England, Scotland, & Ireland descended from the last Parliament of Charles I. Even as it was the Rebellion did introduce a temporary break into the continuity of our constitutional development. The grotesque fiction by which Charles II was looked upon as immediately succeeding Charles I, the effort to blot out from a constitutional point of view every transaction which took place between 1649 & 1660 was due no doubt immediately to the violence of partisanship & of triumphant reaction, but they were also the expression of the instinctive resolution of Englishmen to maintain the historical continuity of their institutions.

3. The Constitution is a work of native production. It is the product of the special *historical conditions* of England.

By this statement is meant that the English Constitution for good & bad is the result of events taking place in England & of the immediate wants & wishes of Englishmen. It is not in any sense a copy of any foreign polity. This cannot be asserted of any or at any rate of most of the constitutions now existing in Europe. They have all of them been more or less consciously influenced by the example of England. The bicameral system of Parliament admits of justification on grounds of policy & expediency but if we ask why it is that almost every modern legislature consists of neither more nor less than two Houses or Chambers, why in short we have not monocameral or tricameral Parliaments the true answer is that it became the fashion to create Parliaments of two Houses because of the fame & the success of the English Constitution under which there have always been two Houses.

If again we ask why it is that English Constitutionalism is an article of purely native manufacture we are driven back to the conditions physical or political which have fixed the course of English progress. The small size of England, the insularity of the country, the easy accessibility of all parts

50 [Oliver Cromwell (1599–1658), lord protector of England, Scotland and Ireland, 1653–8. – Ed.]

thereof, the absence of Roman influence, & above all, the formation at a very early period of a government which could enforce its will throughout the whole land & could therefore establish uniformity of law & uniformity of administration, are some at any rate of the conditions which have given to the Constitution of England its purely English character. Here however we touch upon matters belonging to the province of historians rather than of lawyers, all we need note is that the English Constitution is historical in being in a special sense the immediate result of the conditions which govern English history.[51]

By way of contrast a student may notice the way in which the absence of some among the favourable conditions existing in England arrested the development of Scotch constitutionalism. To begin with there was little essential difference between the political institutions of Scotland & the political institutions of England. In each country you find a mediaeval King & a mediaeval Parliament, in each country there is the mediaeval Church allied in the main politically with the King. Up moreover to the time of

51 Mark the curious absence of all conscious attempts on the part of Englishmen to realise either historical or except in the time of the Puritan revolution, political ideals. Tradition seems in England to have had as little influence as abstract political speculation. Contrast the attempts of the French Revolutionists to carry out theories of equality; contrast also the Italian desire for unity or national independence & the German desire for the renewal of Imperial greatness. Few things are more perplexing than the absence from English history of tradition & its influence. Cromwell made Protestantism triumphant & preserved the unity of what is now the United Kingdom yet in England Cromwell never became a popular hero. There is no Cromwellian legend. The Jacobins, on the other hand, & Napoleon each left behind them a tradition strong enough to affect the whole course of French history. No ministers ever commanded so much popularity as Chatham and his son, yet I doubt whether at Hayes there remains the least recognition of the two Pitts among the people who live there. I have been told that the name of Hampden [John Hampden, 1594–1643, English Parliamentary leader famous for his opposition to King Charles I] is completely forgotten in the village where he lived, & where there are tombs of the family. The only two events which seem to have left something like a tradition are the Gunpowder Plot & the Restoration, & even these are falling more & more out of ordinary memory.

Edward I there was a strong tendency on the part of Scotch Kings & lawyers to imitate the institutions of England yet there was one essential difference. The Scotch King down to the Union of the two countries under James I never possessed anything like the uncontested power which belonged from the time of William the Conqueror to the English Crown. Owing partly to the geographical formation of the country, partly to the existence of Clanship, & partly to other causes, the authority of the Crown was balanced & all but overbalanced by the power of the nobility. Hence there never was established anything like that supremacy of the Royal Courts, which by the time of Edward I at any rate existed in England. Independent jurisdictions belonging to the nobles existed until after 1745, & until 1603 the authority of the Crown was even in the Lowlands extremely precarious & in the Highlands had hardly any existence. Hence two results.

Just because of the independence or unruliness of the nobles, the Scotch Parliament which represents the power of the Crown combined with, or transferred to the Peers & the representatives of the Commons never gained anything like the weight which it possessed in England long before England & Scotland were united under one Crown. To look at the same thing from another point of view the powerlessness of the Scotch Crown made it unnecessary for the nobles & the Commons to unite & place regular & legal limitations on the authority of the King.

When again the movement against the Church of Rome which is known as the Reformation, took place in Scotland, as well as in England the Crown was not in a position to guide & control it. It was carried out by a portion of the nobility & the people & resulted in the formation of a Church system in which the vigorous portions of the nation were more truly represented than in Parliament. It is hardly an exaggeration to say that the Church Assembly was the true representative of the Scotch nation. No doubt the Crown rather than the Parliament came directly into conflict with the Church, but the authority of the Church Assembly was in reality fatal to the authority & development of Parliament. It is well even here to note that the Act of Union gave security to the Scotch Church & whilst it abolished the Parliament which did not represent preserved & safeguarded the Church Assembly which did represent the nation. It was the relation between Church & Parliament which made the Union a possibility & a success. On this point however it is unnecessary to say more here. All that need be noted is that the absence in Scotland of certain favourable conditions which existed in England arrested the development of Scotch constitutionalism. The country with which to compare Scotland in constitutional matters is France. It is quite possible that but for the Union with England the Crown might ultimately have acquired in Scotland something like the authority it gained in France. It is equally possible that had the tendencies which made for Protestantism been as strong in France as in Scotland the French Calvinists might have acquired for the Protestant Church something like the independence & authority which the Scotch Calvinists gained for the Church of Scotland.

B. The Constitution is an *unwritten* Constitution

The expression "unwritten Constitution" is a lax & popular one. It does not mean that considerable parts of the Constitution of England are not to be found in written documents, or even in enactments. The Magna Charta,[52] the Bill of Rights,[53] the Act of Settlement,[54] the Acts of Union are written documents which do contain a great deal of the Constitution.

When we call the Constitution unwritten we mean three things.

52 [See W.S. McKechnie, *Magna Carta* (Glasgow, 1905). – Ed.]

53 [The Bill of Rights, 1689: 'An Act declaring the Rights and Liberties of the Subject and Setleing the Succession of the Crowne'; see Costin & Steven Watson, *op. cit.*, pp. 67–74. – Ed.]

54 [The Act of Settlement, 1701: 'An Act for the further Limitation of the Crown and better security of the Rights and Liberties of the Subject'; see *Ibid.*, pp. 92–6. – Ed.]

1. The articles of the Constitution are not to be found, as are the articles of Constitution of the U.S., in any one definite document or enactment; there is in short no such thing as a written Constitution of England in the sense in which there is a written Constitution of the U.S., of Italy or of Belgium. This however be it remarked is a mere matter of form. If the main provisions of the English Constitution were reduced to the form of an Act passed by Parliament the substance of the Constitution would remain unchanged, provided always that the Constitution Act could be changed or replaced in the same manner as other Acts of Parliament.

2. The articles of the Constitution are to a great extent the result either of legal decisions or of conflicts which resulted in something very like legal decisions.

The fundamental principle for example that the order of the Crown does not justify an illegal act, or that no tax can be imposed except by Act of Parliament may now fairly be deduced from decisions & the Petition of Right or the Bill of Rights comes very near to an authoritative decision on various points of constitutional law.

3. The working of the Constitution depends on understandings or conventions. That this is the fact is undoubted. The rule that if a Ministry is defeated the Cabinet go out of office, the rule that the Queen assents to all Bills passed by Parliament, the rule that the H.L. must ultimately yield to the House of Commons when it is shown that the House represents the will of the nation, are all mere understandings, but they are understandings on which every politician acts & which practically regulate the public life of England. What is the sanction which gives force to these conventions I have elsewhere tried to explain.[55] All that need here be noted is the existence of these conventions. They form a part no doubt of every civilized polity. They have in one or two respects completely modified the working of the Constitution of the U.S. But conventions form a larger part of the

55 A.V. Dicey, *Introduction to the Study of the Law of the Constitution* (London, 1885), ch. 15.

English Constitutional system than of the French or the Italian constitutional system & are apt, it is conceived, to be of less importance under a written than under an unwritten Constitution.

The statement that a constitution is an "unwritten" Constitution is often used as meaning something different from what the words naturally import namely that it is a flexible constitution, or in other words a constitution the articles of which can be changed by the ordinary legislative body or Parliament in the same way in which other laws are changed. This characteristic however of flexibility which belongs to the English Constitution has no essential connection, or but a very slight connection with the fact that a constitutional law of a country is unwritten or, in other words, is not to be found in any one or more definite enactment or enactments. The matter stands thus: where a Constitution is written or enacted the articles thereof are frequently but by no means always "rigid"; they cannot that is to say be changed by the ordinary legislative power in the ordinary course of legislation. Where, on the other hand, a Constitution is unwritten or unenacted, it generally though this does not appear to be necessary, is flexible, its articles that is to say, can be changed by the ordinary legislative body in the ordinary course of legislation. The flexibility however of the English Constitution which is only accidently connected with its being unwritten or unenacted is best considered under our next head.

C. The Constitution is a Parliamentary Constitution

This statement again which appears a very simple one implies much more than the assertion that England in common with almost every modern civilized country has a Parliament by which term we roughly designate any national legislature consisting wholly or in part of persons elected to represent the citizens. When we call the English Constitution Parliamentary we mean certainly to assert that in England laws are passed by a Parliament, but we mean more than this & what is particularly to be noticed, in reality mean to combine together two or three different statements.

Let us try, as in other cases, to analyse all that is implied in the assertion that we have an emphatically parliamentary Constitution.

The English Parliament is a sovereign law making body.[56]

Any law whatever, even the most fundamental laws of the land, can be legally changed by Parliament. No person or body of persons have according to English constitutional law a right to treat an Act of Parliament as invalid. Such an Act may be impolitic, may be immoral, may be unjust, but it cannot be called illegal, unconstitutional or void. Contrast the position of Congress. Any law which exceeds the authority given to Congress under the Constitution is void & will be treated as such by the American Courts. No law, again, to look at the same matter from the negative side is valid in England or throughout the British Empire which is opposed to or contravenes an Act of Parliament. The legislative sovereignty of Parliament is complete & absolute.

The matter may be looked at from another point of view. There is under the English Constitution no way by which the people or the nation can exert supreme legislative authority except by an Act of Parliament. Our Constitution knows of no appeal to the people. There is in England nothing like the so called *plebiscites* of the French Empire or the referendum as it exists in modern Switzerland or though not under that name, in most of the States of America.

The government of England is a parliamentary *Executive*.

The English Executive government is in reality, though not in name, the Cabinet. Now the English Ministry or Cabinet are not, it is true directly chosen by Parliament and a somewhat erroneous impression is conveyed even by the statement now often made that they are indirectly elected by

56 *Ibid.*, chs 1 & 2.

Parliament or rather by the House of Commons. What is true is that the government must consist of "members of Parliament", if we use that term as including members of the House of Lords who command the confidence of the majority of the House of Commons, or, speaking generally, who are the leading men in Parliament among the party who command a majority in the House of Commons. It is therefore in the strictest sense true that the Government is a parliamentary Executive, its members are parliamentary leaders selected from persons who have seats in the House of Commons or the House of Lords; they derive their power from the confidence reposed in them by the House of Commons, & when this confidence is withdrawn they lose office. No King since the revolution of 1688 has even attempted to form an extra parliamentary government, & the very few cases in which a government has been kept for a time in office which did not command a majority in the Commons constitute exactly the exceptions of the kind which proves the rule.

It is natural for Englishmen to imagine that the real legislative authority of Parliament involves the existence of a parliamentary Executive, but, as I shall show in later lectures, one of the most obvious & also one of the most important conclusions impressed upon us by the comparative study of Constitutions is that legislative authority does not necessarily imply executive authority. I will give you but two examples of their severance. The English Parliament itself obtained supreme legislative authority & even legislative sovereignty long before it acquired the right practically to appoint the Executive. None of the Stuarts directly disputed the legislative authority of Parliament; it was not till a considerable time after the Revolution of 1688 that Parliament obtained anything like complete control over the appointment of the Executive. Cabinet government is the growth of modern times. The legislature of Imperial Germany has unlimited or all but unlimited authority in the field of legislation, but it is notorious & admitted that there does not exist in the German Empire a Parliamentary Executive.

Parliament is the centre, so to speak, of English political institutions.

When we call our Constitution parliamentary we have before our minds a fact which it is a little difficult to put into words. We all feel that Parliament & above all the House of Commons as the most powerful member of Parliament plays a part far greater than that which falls to any other English institution.

This is in part the result of history. Century after century the influence of Parliament has increased & the influence of every other power in the State has relatively decreased. The Houses of Parliament & especially the lower House, have, so to speak, become the embodiment of the nation. We can hardly now imagine a state of things under which Parliament did not meet yearly & sit for a large portion of the year. This, be it always remembered, is as time is measured historically a recent phenomenon. No doubt long before the Revolution of 1688 a good King was expected to convene Parliament pretty frequently, but there was no reason to expect anything like the constant sessions of Parliament to which we are accustomed. It moreover has happened in England that every event & every contest has tended in one way or another to increase Parliamentary power. The Restoration marks the greatest reaction which is recorded in the political annals of England, but note that the Restoration was as much the victory of the Parliament as of the King. If Cromwell had put Charles the First to death he had also dissolved by force the only legal Parliament in existence. The Restoration of the King was preceded by the reassembling of the Rump, that is of all that remained of the last legally elected Parliament. Add to this that the Restoration Parliament did not restore the system of administrative government which had existed from the accession of the Tudors to the fall of the Star Chamber. Parliament profited by legislation which as against Parliament had diminished the power of the Crown. Parliament again, as I have before pointed out, has never, excepting the Crown, the power of which it has substantially appropriated, never known any rival authority. The Executive has never been as it still is in Germany, & was for a long time in France, the representative of the nation. Parliament has not in England been checked as is Congress, by State rights which represent the authority of one sovereign & still in one sense of the word, semi sovereign

States. Parliament has never found its power balanced as is the power of the Swiss Federal Assembly, by the direct action of the people.

If you want to see how essentially our government is parliamentary you should consider how totally different would be the abolition of Parliament say in France or in Germany. In England it would mean a total change in our political institutions & in what one may call the habits of ordinary life. In France it would mean nothing like the samething. Parliament was not in strictness abolished but it was, so to speak silenced by Napoleon the Third. It may well be doubted whether outside Paris the change resulting from the *Coup d'etat* was anything like as great as an Englishman would suppose. The Parliament of Prussia was for more than five years not abolished but defied & defied with success by the Crown. If the Parliamentary government of Germany or of Prussia were overthrown – a calamity I may add which is in the highest degree improbable – this would after all mean nothing but a return to a system of which many men now living can remember the existence. The truth is that the Parliament in Prussia for example so far from being the centre of Prussian public life is, so to speak, an institution imported from abroad which does not even as it is work very easily into the arrangements of a monarchical & a military State. There is no constitution in the world which is so strictly Parliamentary as that of England.

D. The modern Constitution of England is a *democratic* Constitution

We may call a polity democratic which has two features. The one is that power should finally reside in the numerical majority of the citizens. This no doubt is not as yet in strictness the case in England. One thing is however certain. Every change which has taken place during the last sixty years & every change proposed for adoption is democratic, i.e. tends to increase the authority given to the majority of the citizens.

The other is the sentiment or conviction which is essentially democratic that the action of the nation in legislation & otherwise ought to be controlled by the will of the majority. This is the substantial meaning of the old phrase "the sovereignty of the people". It is now a principle which admittedly rules the public life of England.

E. The Constitution is a *unitarian* or *unitary* Constitution

A unitarian or as it may be more conveniently called a unitary constitution is contrasted with a federal constitution.[57]

Under a unitary government the sovereign power clearly & visibly, so to speak, resides in some one body, e.g. the King, Parliament, or the like which is supreme throughout the whole of the country. All other authorities whatever power they may possess, can claim nothing but delegated powers; they have no appearance of sovereignty & they are not in any sense part of the sovereign power.

Under a federal government the several States or Cantons, by whatever name they are called, have generally been at one period independent or quasi independent States, the very object of the federal bond is whilst forming them for some purposes into one State or country, to leave them a large amount of independent action, or as it is conveniently called semi-sovereignty. The relation of the States to the central government differs immensely in different federations. In this as in other respects federalism has different forms which admit it is probable of almost infinite variation. Hence the federalism of the United States differs considerably from the federalism of Switzerland & each again differ from the federalism of

57 *Ibid.*, ch. 3 'Parliamentary Sovereignty & Federalism'. See however *Ibid.* (5th edn), p. 413, n. 3.

Germany. Nor would it be impossible to construct a federal union differing in many respects from any existing confederacy. The one point in which every federal government differs from every unitary government is that wherever there is federalism you will find that certain localities or States the union of which makes up the federation, have, as such, State rights whilst under a truly unitary government such as that of France, Italy, or the United Kingdom, there is no such thing known as State rights. To this we may add that the modes in which the independence or quasi independence of the States under a federal form of government is secured are, as far as one can draw inferences from experience two. The several States making up the Confederacy may be bound together by nothing more than a perpetual alliance. They do not in reality acknowledge a common sovereign; there exists no power which can act directly on the citizens of the several States except the power be it Prince or Legislative Assembly, which is supreme in that State. This seem to have been theoretically at any rate the condition of things in the United Provinces, under the German Empire, under the German Confederation between 1815 & 1866, & in the Swiss Confederacy up to 1848 except during the short period when there existed a unitary government, the Helvetic Republic, supported by France. A confederacy of this kind is a body of confederated States, it is not in reality a federal State.

The several States which intend to form a federal State may create a real sovereign power, be it an Assembly or any other body, but the States are in effect themselves members of the sovereign body & hence possess means for protecting their State rights. To this we may add that where a true federal State is thus formed it will generally be found that under the Constitution the different powers of legislation & government are carefully distributed so as to make it difficult for the central government which represents the nation to encroach on the reserved rights of the States or for the States to control in matters concerning the whole nation the action of the central or national governments. The country in which the federal system has been carried out with the greatest elaboration in America. The United States exist in virtue of the Constitution or as we might almost call it the fundamental pact under which a sovereign power is so constituted that it shall at once represent the nation as a whole & the several States. Revolution or violence can change or overthrow any institutions whatever, but as long as the Constitution of the U.S. is respected it is impossible for the States to be deprived of any right given them by the Constitution unless at least three fourths of the States assent thereto. Nor is it at all likely that while the Constitution remains really in force even the attempt to evade the rights of the States can be made unless a very large number of them wish these rights to be curtailed. The outward & visible sign of the acknowledged rights of the States is to be found in the Constitution of the Senate which represents & represents equally every State great & small, & without the assent of the Senate a change in the Constitution is impossible. On this matter it is unnecessary at present to dwell. The point to be forced on the attention of students is that the English Constitution knows nothing of federalism.

This is from one point of view a matter for surprise. The United Kingdom consists of three – if you include Wales one may even say of four – bodies which at one time constituted different countries. It might have been expected *a priori* that the union of these countries should it ever take place, would assume a federal form. As a matter of fact nothing of the sort has happened. This is the more noteworthy because the people of England, Wales, Scotland & Ireland have been by no means so completely fused into one undistinguishable body as the inhabitants of the different provinces, say, of France. The explanation of a singular phenomenon is probably to be found in the history of England. From the time of the Norman Conquest the central government was stronger in England than in almost any other European country. The Crown, as represented by the Courts, was supreme throughout the whole land. The power of the Crown was first encroached upon by, next shared with, & lastly, transferred in effect to, Parliament. But the process by which Parliamentary authority grew up had no tendency whatever to alter the unitary character of the Constitution. The very contests with the Crown led to union among every class of the people. The Houses of Parliament never relied upon local rights or the privileges of particular "Estates". In the very height of civil war they asserted quite as strenuously as the Crown the sovereignty of the nation. The first union with England was the complete legal fusion of Wales with the rest of the country under Henry VIII, but union took the form of fusion not of alliance when at the beginning of the 18th century union with Scotland became an urgent necessity English statesmen & England generally had become thoroughly accustomed to the idea of an incorporative as contrasted with a federal union and in 1706 the English Commissioners for negotiating the terms on which the two Kingdoms should be united absolutely refused to entertain any idea of constituting a federation. "The English offered an article containing the fundamental principles of the treaty – one Kingdom with a new name, one Parliament & a destination of the new Crown according to the Act of Succession. It was felt that on the adoption or rejection of this proposition the fate of the whole project depended". When nearly a century later the Act of Union with Ireland was carried, the Treaty of Union with Scotland was an authoritative precedent which there was neither the wish nor the intention to neglect. A large party in Ireland objected to the policy of union but no one, I conceive, in 1800 whether he were a friend or an opponent of the Union, advocated federalism.

The Constitution of the United Kingdom therefore though formed by the combination under one polity of three countries politically & geographically distinct bears no trace of a federal character. It is emphatically a unitary Constitution.

3

Comparison between English & other Executives: Parliamentary & non-Parliamentary Executives

[No date]

Parliamentary government in a wide sense of that term has during the last hundred years become common to almost all civilised States. For in every European country except Turkey & Russia, there exists an Assembly more or less elective which exercises more or less of legislative authority. In England further Parliamentary government in this sense of the term has existed for centuries, let us say roughly from the time of Edward I. But though all civilized governments are now in a sense Parliamentary it has not been enough noticed that under the general head Parliamentary government are included two distinct types of government which are differentiated from one another according to the relation between the executive body & the legislative body.

The Executive may consist of a person or body of persons which are in fact appointed & dismissible, [by] the legislature. This may be termed a Parliamentary Executive. The Executive again may be a person or body of persons not appointed or dismissible by the legislature. This may be termed an extra-parliamentary Executive.

If we divide constitutions according to the relation between the executive & the legislature we obtain a classification which gives curious results because it exhibits the point of likeness between Constitutions apparently dissimilar from each other & the point of difference between Constitutions in which may be traced a strong family likeness.

Under Constitutions with parliamentary Executives we may bring the modern British Constitution & subject to some limitations all Constitutional monarchies, all the Constitutions of such British colonies as enjoy representative government & also the existing French Republic which curiously enough was intended by its founders to possess a more or less extra-parliamentary Executive whilst the course of events has turned the government of the Republic into one of the extremest forms of parliamentary executive. In the same class we must number the Republic of France during the existence of the Convention & the English Commonwealth from the death of Charles I until the creation of the Protectorate.

Under Constitutions with extra-parliamentary executives we must bring the U.S., the German Empire, the Napoleonic Empire under all its different forms prior to 1815 & again between 1852 and 1870. Under the same head ought to be classed the old monarchy of England till certainly as late as 1688, & in truth till a later period, and also the government of the Protector from 1653 to 1658.

For reasons which will become more apparent in the course of this lecture we shall find more than one Constitution as to which it may be a fair question whether its government is to be counted as a Parliamentary or an extra-parliamentary executive. This is true for example of the Swiss Confederation & possibly of some nominally constitutional monarchies. In this lecture I propose first to consider what is meant by a parliamentary executive, to exhibit to you its two main types, & to show you how the British Constitution in this as in other instances has preserved throughout centuries an almost unchanged form whilst in reality it has gone through an extraordinary transformation so as to have passed from the class of Constitutions whereof the Executive is extra-parliamentary into the class of Constitutions whereof the Executive is more strictly parliamentary than the government of any country except possibly that of modern France. I shall then commence the examination by way of contrast & comparison of polities whereof the government has an extra parliamentary character.

It is always well to vary from time to time the phrases in which a doctrine or fact is expressed. This course guards us to some extent against the danger of being the slaves of names. I therefore will sum up before proceeding further the result of the distinction on which I am insisting in the following form. In England, France, etc., there exists not only parliamentary government but also government by parliament. In the U.S. & the German Empire government by parliament does not exist though there does exist parliamentary government.

A. Constitutions with a Parliamentary Executive

An elective legislative Assembly or parliament has often in different countries & times attempted with more or less success to get into its hands the functions of the executive government.

Experience seems to show that practically such a legislative assembly which aims at exercising executive functions must take one of two courses. It must either, directly appoint committees from among its own body or else whilst not attempting directly to carry on the administration, obtain a more or less predominant voice in the appointment of executive officers who when appointed may carry on the work of administration without constant reference to Parliament. To put the same thing in other words government by parliament may either mean administration by committee, or what we in England call Cabinet government.

Government by Committees

The simplest, & as it would at first sight appear the most effective form in which an assembly too large to form of itself an executive body can carry on the administrative business of a great nation is to appoint committees of its own members for the management of different affairs. This was the course taken on two celebrated occasions by two celebrated legislatures. The Long Parliament after the defeat of the King & the French Convention during the whole time of its existence governed through Committees. This system though natural & to appearance effective, has at least two defects. The first is that it does not tend to produce good and successful administration. Government by a body of Committees means government through rival and clashing authorities. Unless as happened during the Reign of Terror, a small body of men concentrate the authority of the ruling legislature in their own hands government by committees must almost of necessity be weak & ineffective government.

A second defect is that government by parliamentary committees violates the soundest part of Montesquieu's[58] doctrine enjoining the separation of powers. It is plain that when a supreme legislature tries to govern directly through the agency of committees legislative judicial, & executive powers are blended together. The legislature is law maker, judge, & executioner in one, & is all but certain to exhibit in a short time all the worst features of a tyrant.

This point is well illustrated by Paley. "For the sake of illustration", he writes "let it be supposed, in this country, either that, parliaments being laid aside, the Courts of Westminster Hall made their own laws, or that the two Houses of Parliament, with the King at their head, tried & decided causes at their bar; it is evident, in the first place, that the decisions of such a judicature would be so many laws; and, in the second place, that, when the parties & the interests to be affected by the law were known, the inclinations of the law-makers would inevitably attach to one side or the other; & that, where there were neither any fixed rules to regulate their determinations, nor any superior power to control their proceedings, these inclinations would interfere with the integrity of public justice. The consequence of which must be, that the subjects of such a Constitution would live either

58 [Montesquieu, Charles-Louis de Secondat (1689–1755), French political philosopher; major work: *The Spirit of Laws* (1750). – Ed.]

without any constant laws, that is, without any known pre-established rules of adjudication whatever; or under laws made for particular cases and particular persons, & partaking of the contradictions & iniquity of the motives to which they owed their origin".[59]

The history both of the Long Parliament & of the Convention exactly confirms the truth of the doctrine laid down in this passage. The experience of other countries tells the same way. Direct government by parliament through committees, & it is the only way by which a large assembly can attempt direct government is certain to promote injustice.

Cabinet government

The second method by which an assembly can exercise executive power is by leaving large powers to the executive to be exercised by it at its own discretion but at the same time keeping in the assembly's own hands the means of appointing, controlling, & criticising the executive.

This is the course of action which by a sort of instinctive policy the British Parliament has for centuries pursued. Neither of the Houses singly, nor both of them acting together have ever except during revolutionary periods effected to give direct commands to any executive officer. Neither the House of Commons nor the House of Lords can appoint or give directions to either a judge or a policeman. What the Houses have done is at first in fact & then more or less nominally to leave the executive in the hands of the King & his officers, and to leave the ministry or government the exercise of all the royal prerogatives. But at the same time to obtain by degrees first the right of controlling the policy of the government, secondly the right that ministers should as a rule be members of the Houses of Parliament & thirdly the right of dismissing ministers who were not supported by the

59 William Paley, *The Principles of Moral and Political Philosophy* (London, 1785), Book VI, ch. viii.

House of Commons, & lastly, in effect of designating to the Crown by an indirect process who should be appointed minister.

In the modern British executive one must therefore carefully distinguish *form* from *substance.*

In *form* the Cabinet are the servants of the Crown through whom the Crown's prerogatives are exercised & who are appointed & dismissed by the Crown.

In *fact* the Cabinet are a body chosen from among the members of the two Houses, who though in constant consultation with the Crown are really in their main the servants of Parliament. The Cabinet exercise the royal prerogatives in accordance with the general wish of Parliament. They are speaking generally both appointed & dismissed by Parliament or in fact by the House of Commons.

The system of government by Parliament has in the course of its development passed through several stages.

First. The establishment of Parliament's exclusive right of *legislation.*

Secondly. The establishment of the right of Parliament to criticise & *control* the acts of the Kings *servants* or ministers.

Thirdly. Parliament's right in extreme cases to *drive* a *minister from power.*

Fourthly. The principle that ministers must be *members* of one or other of the Houses of Parliament.

Fifthly. Parliament's right, or in effect the right of the House of Commons to dismiss & lastly to *appoint* or *elect* the ministry.

I have tried to give the development of these rights or powers in their historical order. You will observe that the right of *appointment* is placed subsequently to the right of dismissal; this is because the logical & the historical order of things differ. The House of Commons could in substance dismiss Walpole.[60] The House of Commons could not determine

60 [Sir Robert Walpole (1676–1745), prime minister, 1721–42. – Ed.]

who should be Walpole's successor. One of the points contested between George III & the "Orthodox Whigs" if so we may call them, represented by Rockingham[61] & inspired by Burke[62] was the right of appointment, especially to the Premiership. The King maintained & to a certain extent made good his right to choose if not the party who should hold office, at any rate the member of that party who should be Premier. The Rockingham Whigs maintained that the party or connection had the right to nominate the Prime Minister.

Let it be remarked that even down to the present day the right of indirect appointment or even of dismissal by the House of Commons is not absolutely established by constitutional custom.

This right is subject to one more or less *formal* & to another very *real* check. The formal limitation is that the Crown can exercise a certain though indefinite amount of choice in the selection of the Premier. Nor can anyone who recalls to his mind the events of 1839 deny that under peculiar circumstances the Crown can keep in office ministers who hardly command the support of the House of Commons.

The material & very real check consists of a Cabinet's power with the assent of the Crown, of appealing by means of a dissolution from Parliament to the constituencies.

In 1857 Parliament condemned but the electors supported the government of Lord Palmerston.[63]

In 1874 Parliament still supported, but the electors, or, as the expression goes, the country, did not support the government of Mr Gladstone.

In each case the will of the country was decisive.

61 [Lord Rockingham (1730–82), first lord of the treasury, 1765–6. – Ed.]

62 [Edmund Burke (1729–97), politician and author; see Paul Langford (ed.), *The Writings and Speeches of Edmund Burke* (9 vols, Oxford, 1981–2000). – Ed.]

63 [Henry John Temple, 3rd Viscount Palmerston (1784–1865), prime minister, 1855–8, 1859–65. – Ed.]

An English Cabinet therefore is a strictly Parliamentary executive indirectly appointed & dismissed by the vote of the House of Commons subject at any rate as to dismissal, to more or less formal control by the Crown & to real control by the electors, or the country.

The oddity of the thing is that if you look to matters of form, the English Cabinet is an extra-parliamentary executive. If you look at the substance it is all but a completely Parliamentary executive. I purposely use the words "all but" in order to impress upon you that authorities external to the Houses of Parliament do exercise a certain control over the executive, namely the Crown, & the country, or the electors.

This control you will say, is inherent in the nature of things. The remark is plausible but unsound. We can see before our eyes if we look across the Channel, a more thoroughly Parliamentary form of government than that of England. In France you have an executive dependent all but entirely for its existence & its power, upon the Chambers, and the authority of the Chambers is nearly freed from the checks which exist under the English Constitution.

The matter is well worth a moment's attention. The French President of the Republic is elected for 7 years by the two Houses of the National Assembly sitting together as what is called a Congress. The President was meant according to the theory of the Constitution to hold his office for 7 years term without any risk of dismissal by Parliament. He like an English King, appoints the ministry, he further, unlike an English King, often if not always takes part in the meetings of the Cabinet. But the French President can no more than an English King carry on the government unless his ministers have the support of Parliament. He further is as the experience of President Grevy[64] proved, in fact though not in theory dismissible by the legislature. The French Parliament is therefore free in the appointment or dismissal of ministers from such control as may be exercised in England by the authority of the Crown.

64 [Jules Grévy (1807–91), French republican president, 1879–87. – Ed.]

A French Parliament is also all but free from the control which is exercised in England by the country when appealed to by means of a dissolution. In order that the French National Assembly may be dissolved the assent both of the President & of the Senate must be obtained. The President be it remarked is a nominee of the Assembly & the Senate is one portion of the Assembly. Parliament therefore can determine whether it be dissolved or not, & the right of dissolution may thus be refused to a ministry who on appeal to the country could undoubtedly secure the support of a Parliamentary majority. Gambetta's[65] chance of remaining and becoming head of the government of France and probably to have become the most powerful Minister of the time was lost because neither the President nor the Senate would allow him to dissolve Parliament. It is true that in France Parliament lasts for a period only of four years. It is likely therefore that a public man who say in 1890 commands the confidence of the country will by or before 1894, find himself at the head of a Parliamentary majority. This likelihood however is no certainty. Who can say whether if in 1783 Pitt[66] had been prevented from immediately consulting the country or if in 1857 Parliament had been unable to dissolve, either Minister would ever have been in command of a Parliamentary majority?

In any case the point to be noted is that in France the Cabinet system of government by Parliament has advanced a stage beyond the point which it has reached in England. A newly elected Assembly has the all but unlimited power of appointing & dismissing ministries. Foreigners cannot say whether this right be or be not abused. It is assuredly employed with great freedom.

Under the French Republic a form of government which may be nominally termed Presidential turns out on examination to be in reality an extreme form of government by Parliament, which gives the appointment

65 [Leon Gambetta (1838–82), French republican statesman, premier, 1881–2. – Ed.]

66 [William Pitt (1759–1806), 'Pitt the younger', prime minister, 1783–1801, 1804–6. – Ed.]

of the executive more completely into the hands of an elective legislature than is the case under the constitutional monarchy of England.

In many on the other hand, if not all of the constitutional monarchies which exist or have existed on the Continent it will be found on examination that the copy of English constitutionalism (at any rate as it at present exists) is imperfect & that the Cabinet is not so truly a Parliamentary executive as it is with us.

Naturally enough the imitators of the English Constitution have adopted its form more easily than its essence: a monarch who reigns but does not govern is a ruler hardly suited for countries going through or emerging from revolutions. Hence continental constitutionalists have always been met by the difficulty of fixing the true share of a constitutional monarch in the appointment of the cabinet & in the acts of the executive. Look for a moment at France between 1815 and 1848. Neither Louis XVIII nor Charles X, nor Louis Philippe were constitutional monarchs of the modern English type. Of these the first & the last never disputed the exclusive authority of Parliament in matters of legislation. Louis Philippe at any rate never denied that a ministry could not last which lacked the support of a Parliamentary majority. But the head of the Orleans dynasty was no more inclined than either of his predecessors to admit that he was not himself a part, & we may say a predominant part of the executive government. Louis XVIII and Louis Philippe each were present at Cabinet meetings; each of them was a real head of the government, Louis Philippe perhaps more truly than his cousin. He occupied in reality under very different circumstances & by the use of very different means much the position claimed for himself by George III. He acquiesced in Parliamentary institutions but he remained as long as he sat on the throne a real head of the executive. George III used to say of himself that he was a Revolutionary Whig. The dictum had in it more truth than perhaps it was intended to contain. His Majesty's effort throughout his reign was really though unconsciously the restoration of the Crown to the position it occupied in the time of William & of Anne. The legislative authority & the political control of Parliament was then fully admitted. But the staunchest revolutionary Whig would not have denied that the King or Queen was the head of the government. That the executive of England was the King was the theory of Blackstone; in the time of William or of Anne constitutional theory & constitutional fact coincided. Mr Morley's[67] recent studies have made clear to all the world what everyone before knew vaguely, that Cabinet government, i.e. the supremacy of a Parliamentary executive, did not exist even in outline till the accession of the House of Hanover.

B. Constitutions with an extra-parliamentary executive

Governments which are not parliamentary executives have all one negative quality in common: they are none of them appointed by the legislature of the country where they exist.

They may however be roughly divided into two classes. They may be popular executives, i.e. governments appointed not by the legislature but by popular election, such for example is the American Presidency. They may be governments consisting of, or appointed by some monarch such for example is the Imperial Executive of Germany, or the royal Cabinet of Prussia.

The fact it may be noted which makes it possible for an extra-parliamentary executive to exist, is that even in countries where there is an elective legislature the people or the classes who in the last resort guide the people will on some matters & within certain limits either by their votes or their arms support the executive, be he President or Emperor, against the legislative body. This is a point which Englishmen of the 19th century find it hard to understand. They can easily conceive of an absolute monarch who combines in his own hands the authority of a legislator & of the head of the

67 [John Morley (1838–1923), historian, liberal politician. – Ed.]

executive, or to put the thing plainly of a Commander in Chief. They can understand, for they live under the rule of, a practically sovereign legislature, but what they find it extremely difficult to understand is that side by side with a King or President who is the real head of the State, & who exercises real executive powers there shall exist a true legislature with real legislative powers, or in other words with real authority to make laws. Englishmen cannot believe as regards executive & legislative authority in any real "separation of powers". The difficulty is caused by two circumstances – first, the want of experience of a Constitution where this kind of division is clearly drawn, secondly, a logical puzzle of the following kind: a legislature, it is argued, which can pass laws & can really legislate & *a fortiori* a legislature which under the form of law making imposes taxes can always either by means of direct legislation or by cutting short the supplies, obtain command of the executive government. Wherever therefore there is a real parliament there is also under one name or another, a parliamentary government. The fallacy of this argument is twofold. Its formal flaw is that a real legislature, such for example as the American Congress need not under the articles of the Constitution have unlimited legislative authority. Its laws may be invalid when they touch the sphere of the executive. The more serious or substantial error is that a nation may without any inconsistency be prepared to obey the legislature whilst acting within a particular sphere & be prepared to obey the executive whilst acting within another sphere. There is no logical inconsistency in the American people being willing to obey the President as regards appointments to office & the like, and being willing to obey Congress as regards laws within the competence of Congress. The distinct sphere of the two powers which are established in the U.S. by a written Constitution may exist & have existed in other countries by virtue of custom. No doubt it is impossible either by law or custom so to discriminate between executive & legislative powers that the authority of the government & the legislature shall never clash. Who it may be asked, will the nation then obey? No rule can be *a priori* established. Half the nation may obey the legislature, half the government. What in a civilized country is even more probable is that the nation will obey the authority which in the judgement of sensible men is least responsible for the collision. In any case the nation are extremely likely to insist in a country where the separation of powers is an accepted feature of political life that the separation shall be preserved, & directly or indirectly to punish the authority whether legislative or executive which has violated a fundamental constitutional principle. All this may savour of digression; it is a digression however necessitated or excused by the importance of bringing home to Englishmen the often neglected fact that there is no reason in the nature of things why a true parliament or legislature should not co-exist with a true extra-parliamentary executive.

As such extra parliamentary executive may be either elective or hereditary we may roughly divide governments belonging to this class into – first, presidential governments, secondly, monarchical governments. The best type of the one is found in the U.S., a good if not the best type of the other is found in the German Empire.

Presidential executive

The presidency of the U.S. is the type of presidential government.[68] The President is under a complicated system with which we need not trouble ourselves, in effect elected by the people of the U.S. This is not exactly what you will find written in the Constitution which will tell you that each of the States elect certain electors & that the electors select the president. But the electors are now nothing better than ballot balls; they are every one of them elected to choose a particular man say Cleveland[69] or Harrison,[70] as President & it would be the grossest breach of public honour which a man could commit to vote for any other person than the presidential candidate whom he was chosen to elect. Under certain exceptional circumstances a

68 See Bryce, *op. cit.*, vol. I, pp. 38–214.

69 [Grover Cleveland (1837–1908), president of the US, 1893–97. – Ed.]

70 [William Harrison (1773–1841), president of the US, 1841. – Ed.]

President might be chosen by Congress. But these circumstances have never arisen since the foundation of the Union & are not very likely to arise. Dismiss from your minds therefore all idea that the President is nominated by Congress. He is chosen by the people, not by the legislature; he represents the nation as truly as Congress, perhaps more truly.

The President is elected for 4 years; during his tenure of office he cannot be dismissed. No vote of Congress can deprive him of his position. He is re-eligible. He may be and as a matter of fact sometimes is, re-elected at the end of his term for a second Presidential period. Not a word in the Constitution forbids or discourages constant re-election. But a custom which has now the force of law prohibits a President from being re-elected more than once. A President's tenure of office in short is a certain 4 years & a just possible 4 years tenure. But no man ever has, & we may safely say that as things now stand, no man ever will hold the presidency for more than 8 years. The immediate point however for you to notice is not so much the length of time for which, but the conditions on which he holds power. The creation & the continuance of his authority is absolutely independent of Congress. The President may be a free trader; Congress may be filled by Protectionists. The President may favour an aggressive foreign policy, the majority in Congress may hold that no national triumph is worth the sacrifice of peace. But whether the Congress & the President differ or agree they must somehow get on together. Disagreement is not only possible, but highly probable. The President & Congress in America have more than once carried on with each other war to the knife, in so far as war was possible within the limits of the Constitution.

The President is a real head of the Government. He has been called a George the Third elected for 4 years. He has, be it added, many powers which George III claimed in theory but could only occasionally exercise in practice.

i. The President is in a real & effective sense the head of the executive; he appoints officials subject to the approval of the Senate; he is commander-in-chief in the sense that he can really appoint the general in command &

can give directions as to what the general shall do. (Constitution, art. 1, s. 2) He has power to grant pardons, & in matter of fact Lincoln's power of pardoning military offenders during the civil war was at times exerted in a way which the generals thought inconsistent with army discipline.

ii. He has a suspensive veto on legislation. He may send back a bill for reconsideration by the two Houses & unless it again passes each House by a 2/3rds majority the bill does not become law. This veto is not an obsolete prerogative but an increasingly exercised power (Constitution, art 1, s. 7).

iii. He can make treaties with the assent of the Senate (Constitution, art 2, s. 2).

iv. He is irremovable except on impeachment for treason & other high crimes and misdemeanours.

v. The exercise of his power is not impeded by the necessity of having a Parliamentary Cabinet.

The so called Cabinet is a body of Seven Ministers appointed by the President, subject to the assent of the Senate which is never refused. They are simply departmental officers who have no seats in Congress, & cannot address Congress. They are in no sense Parliamentary leaders. None of them is a Premier & they do not act collectively. A seat in the Cabinet is not now, as it once was, a stepping stone to the Presidency. The President is responsible, the Minister is practically irresponsible.[71]

"In America the administration does not work as a whole. It is not a whole. It is group of persons each individually dependent upon & answerable to the President but with no joint policy, no collective responsibility".[72]

N.B. The President can no more dissolve Congress than Congress can remove the President.

71 See Bryce, *op. cit.*, pp. 86–96.

72 See Bryce, *Ibid.*, for contrast between English & American Cabinet.

The French Presidential Republic of 1848 was, as regards the Executive, modelled to a certain extent on the American Constitution.

The President was elected by the whole French people for four years; he was not re-eligible.

1. He had the ordinary powers of a constitutional King except in regard to legislation.
2. He had no veto but had the right of sending back a law to the Assembly for reconsideration (Constitution, art. 59).
3. He had the power to appoint and dismiss Ministers as well as commanders-in-chief, etc.
4. His acts needed ministerial countersignature.
5. The Ministers had a right to enter and speak in the National Assembly. Hence the Ministers might either be, or not be, members of the Assembly.
6. The Ministry was a Cabinet in the English sense of the term, but I conceive that the President could take part in the Cabinet meetings.

N.B. The French Republican Constitution constituted a curious & inconsistent mixture of the system of Presidential government & of Cabinet government.

Authority of President rivalled authority of legislature. In so far he was an extra-parliamentary Executive.

The President's Ministers on the other hand were practically, if not members of, dependent upon the Assembly & therefore constituted a Parliamentary executive.

Only consistent plans would have been either to make President appointed by Assembly, as under present Republic, or to keep Ministers outside the Assembly as in America.

Under French Imperial government whatever its form, an essential feature was that the Emperor should be the real head of the Executive & that the executive body should be in the strictest sense extra-parliamentary.

There were Ministers but there was no Ministry or Cabinet (See e.g. Constitution 1852, Lit. III, s. 13, art. 13) for

1. The Ministers are each responsible to the President.
2. They are each departmental Ministers.
3. They have no joint responsibility.
4. They are not members of the legislature (Constitution, art. 44).
5. The Ministers do not as such, defend laws before the Assembly (Constitution, arts 50, 51).
6. The President is responsible to the French people.

These provisions are noteworthy as they constitute the exact negation of Cabinet government.

It should be noted that the gradual modifications of the Imperial government, e.g. by the decree of 19 Jan. 1867, are all approximations towards Cabinet government, & at every step there became apparent the contradiction between the parliamentary & the extra-parliamentary system, especially the law of 8 Sept. 1869. The plain truth is that the two systems are logically & practically irreconcilable. Of their respective merits & demerits I hope to say something in the next lecture. Meanwhile let me take a last example of an extra-parliamentary executive from the German Empire. The real & effective head of the Imperial government. [Page missing.]

4

Cromwellian Constitution of 1653

[No date]

A. Cromwellian Constitution of 1653[73]

In my last lecture I explained the exact difference between constitutions which have a parliamentary executive and constitutions which have an extra-parliamentary executive.

As types of the one kind of polity I selected the monarchical constitution of modem England and the Republican constitution of modern France.

As types of the other kind of polity I selected the United States, the French Republic of 1848, and the existing German Empire.

I further pointed out in the course of my lecture that the English Constitution had at one time been a constitution with an extra-parliamentary executive and still was so in form but that under a curious process of development it had at last become a constitution with a more completely parliamentary executive than any existing Commonwealth unless it be the French Republic.

I propose tonight to carry the system of comparison on which this course of lectures is based a step further and compare the position of the executive in England of the 19th century with the position of the executive under what we may call the great Puritan Constitution of 1653, or in

73 See Gardiner, *Documents of Puritan Revolution*, *op. cit.*, pp. 271, 314.

other words with the constitution embodied in the so-called Instrument of Government.

Whilst however my main subject is to contrast the extra-parliamentary executive created by the Instrument of Government with the parliamentary executive or Cabinet which taken in combination with the Crown forms the true executive government of modern England I shall avail myself of this opportunity to bring out as clearly as I can the essential differences between the Cromwellian constitution of 1653 and the Victorian Constitution of 1890.

For the present purpose you need not trouble yourselves with the steps by which historically the constitution of 1653 came into being. It was in fact influenced as is supposed to a great extent by the idea of Ireton.[74] It was framed by Cromwell and what we may call the Cromwellian Republicans, after the so called Barebone's Parliament[75] had resigned its authority to Cromwell.

Let us examine and criticise the Constitution of 1653 not as historians but rather as legists just as we should criticise, say the Constitution of the US.

The constitution of 1653 possesses besides its inherent merits the special interest that it is the earliest of that long series of written constitutions of which during the last hundred years, so many have been created and so few have stood the test of time.

For our present purpose this Constitution has the further claim to our attention that it is an elaborate attempt to create for the government of

74 [Henry Ireton (1611–51), parliamentarian army officer, regicide, married Cromwell's daughter. – Ed.]

75 [A council of officers headed by Cromwell to run civil government and foreign policy on a day-to-day basis. They met in the Commons chamber, announcing they were a parliament. One of the fanatic members of this council was the Baptist Praisegod Barbon. Hence the name. – Ed.]

England at once a real legislative assembly or Parliament and also a strong extra-parliamentary executive.

Let us note the following features in the Constitution of the Protectorate. They have curious points both of contrast and of similarity with the parliamentary Constitution of today.

I. The Lord Protector.

The Protector, Oliver Cromwell, is appointed for life, but the Protectorship unlike the Kingship, is elective and not hereditary. After Cromwell's death, succeeding Protectors are to be elected for life by the Council (see Instruments of Government, art. 3 to 6). He is to be the real head, the real executive power. All writs run in his name, all honours and offices are at his disposal. He has the right of pardon except in case of murder and treason. He has with the consent of Parliament the control of all military and naval forces. He is to govern by the advice of the Council in accordance with the Constitution (i.e. with the Instrument itself) and with the laws. A revenue is secured from customs for the maintenance of a standing army of 10,000 horse and 20,000 foot and also a revenue of £ 200,000 for the necessary expenses of government. This whole revenue cannot be taken away or diminished but with the consent both of the Protector and Parliament (*Ibid.* arts 27, 28 and 30). This revenue being secured, no other tax or charge can be imposed but by common consent in Parliament (art. 6) The laws it is [*sic*] provided are not to be altered, suspended, abrogated, or repealed without the consent of Parliament.

The Protector is therefore under the Instrument a ruler who holds his office for life but who must rule in accordance with law. He is however a real ruler The powers given him and the revenues secured to him, place him beyond that indirect control of Parliament, which has gradually transferred to the House of Commons the prerogatives of the Crown.

His position has a close resemblance to that of an American president. It is in substance though not in form like the position of a German Emperor. The Protector, like the Emperor, is a real ruler whose authority is protected against Parliamentary encroachment. But the Protector like the German Emperor is a ruler bound by the Constitution and by the law of the land. Neither one or the other has independent powers of legislation though both are in effect part of the legislature. Protector and Emperor alike though possessing large executive powers, are under the Constitution bound to respect the legislative authority of an elective assembly or Parliament. (Compare Masson, 542).

II. The Council.

(*Instruments*, arts 2–5, 25–27, 30, 32)

The Council are a permanent body, named by the Instrument itself (*Instruments*, arts 4, 25, 26) of 15 persons and as many more not exceeding 6, as Protector and the Council should [?] add before the meeting of the first Parliament.

1. The members of the Council are appointed for life, but may be removed for misconduct, e.g. corruption.

2. New members are appointed from six nominated by Parliament out of which council elect two and from these Protector selects one.

3. The council advise Protector on points of government (*Instruments* art 5).

4. Protector with the consent of the Council has power of temporary legislation (ordinances) (*Instruments* art. 30).

5. Council on death of Protector elect successor and until election carry on Government.

The Council seems to be the Privy Council with larger and more definite powers especially of legislation than were possessed by the Privy Council.

It rather resembles the American Senate which originally consisted of only 26 persons. It was not a Cabinet, for it could not be dismissed nor directly elected by Parliament. But owing to its indirect connection with Parliament it could not have ultimately failed to represent Parliamentary opinion.

Masson notes that Cromwell had never any difficulties with his Council.

The Parliament consists of one House of 400 members for England and Wales and 30 each for Ireland and Scotland. Semble [*sic*] it was intended that Jersey and Guernsey should be also represented (*Instruments* art. 10).

i. Parliament is triennial, i.e. to meet every third year.
ii. Cannot be adjourned, prorogued, or dissolved without consent, during five months from day of meeting (*Instruments* art. 8).
iii. The seats are distributed under the Instrument.
iv. The electors are all persons possessed of estate real or personal to the value of £ 200 and not within certain exceptions, all of which are temporary except that excluding Roman catholics.
v. Parliament may be summoned at intermediate periods by Protector with advice of Council and Parliament must be summoned in case of war with foreign power.
vi. All bills agreed to by Parliament to be presented to Protector for consent. If within 20 days he does not consent, or satisfy Parliament they become law.
vii. Certain matters are beyond legislative authority of Parliament.

The constitution is what is now called a rigid constitution, but the degree of rigidity is rather uncertain.

According to Gardiner, the Instrument contains no means for its own legal alteration. This conclusion is based on art. 24. The inference seems to me doubtful. The Instrument criticised from a merely legal point of view may, it is submitted, be interpreted as dividing laws into three classes.

(a) Laws which may be passed by Parliament without the consent of the Protector. Under this lead come all laws which do not affect the Instrument of government, or as we should now say the articles of the Constitution.

(b) Laws which may be passed by Parliament with the consent of the Protector, i.e. laws which affect the Instrument of Government generally (*Instruments* art. 24).

(c) Laws which cannot be passed at all, i.e. laws which affect Christian liberty as provided for in arts 35–38, or which affect the sale of lands, the security of the public debt etc. provided for by Acts of Parliament and referred to in art. 39.

If this view be correct the Constitution is by no means excessively rigid. Parliament has complete control over ordinary legislation. Parliament with the consent of the Protector, can alter most parts of the Constitution. The only thing[s] made unchangeable are the provisions securing the right of religious liberty and sales etc. carried out under the authority of Parliament.

We have therefore in the Cromwellian constitution of 1653 a form of government which throws a curious light on modem English constitutionalism from two points of view.

First, it shows that the constitutional idea of the Commonwealth men were in some respects essentially different from the idea of the Whigs who in 1689 finally expelled the Stuarts, and ultimately laid the foundation of our modern Parliamentary system. These are some of the chief points of contrast:

(1) Under the Protectorate the Executive was a body which though slightly connected with Parliament was in the strict sense extra-parliamentary. The Protector and his successors were not appointed by Parliament. Neither the Protector nor the Council could be removed by Parliament. A fixed revenue moreover was secured to the executive and also an army which were placed beyond Parliamentary control.

(2) The Council formed a body of highly paid officials – the salary, according to Mr Masson, of each Councillor was equivalent in our money to about £3,500 a year – who were to a certain extent independent at once of the Protector and of Parliament. I know of no constitutional body which the Council so nearly resembles as the American Senate. But the power and the independence of the Councillors exceeded that of the United States Senators. The Council and the Protector had moreover authority to issue in the absence of Parliament, what we may call Ordinances which remained in force unless in some way revoked by Parliament (*Instruments*, art. 30).

(3) The Legislature on the other hand, is an independent legislative body, at once more powerful and less powerful than the Houses of Parliament under the Stuarts. The legislature is more powerful than the Houses in the 17th century because the Cromwellian Parliament must be convoked at least once every three years, cannot for 5 months be dissolved without own consent, has an indirect share in the nomination of council and can, except on certain topics, pass laws by its own authority. The Cromwellian legislature is however less powerful than the two Houses because the Protector and Council are an independent government, are provided with revenue and an army and are disconnected with the legislature and because the legislature's power to change the constitution either does not exist or is at any rate limited in regard to certain topics. The legislature, in short, is bound by the constitution. The Constitution is, to use modern expression, based on a separation of powers. [*Crossed out in blue crayon*: Note particularly that the Parliamentarian opposition in the Parliament summoned under the Instrument of government 1853, attempted in their proposed scheme Bill of November 1654 to amend the Instrument in favour of the Parliament.]

(4) The Constitution recognises fundamental and unchangeable laws (*Instruments* art. 24) and possibly (makes the whole Constitution unchangeable by any recognised process). It is worth notice that the Constitutional Bill of Cromwell's first Parliament, in so far as it deviates from the Instrument is all in favour of Parliamentary power. Thus: the Constitution is made amendable by Parliament (Cap. II); the election of Protector is, if

Parliament be sitting, placed in the hands of Parliament; the approval of persons nominated to the Council is placed in the hands of Parliament; it is further not quite clear whether any articles whatever of the Constitution are placed beyond the competence of Parliament to deal with them.

The differences between the Instrument of Government of the Parliamentary Constitutional Bill strike a reader at first sight as comparatively trifling. There is however one essential difference which it is easy to underrate. Under the Instrument of Government the Parliament is the creature of the Constitution; under the Bill the Constitution is the creature of Parliament. To have passed the bill would have been in effect a denial of Cromwell's authority under the Instrument. Both the Instrument of Government and the constitutional Bill rest however on ideas foreign to the Whig notion of. Parliamentary government. They both substitute a written for an unwritten Constitution, they both place a strong and non-parliamentary executive side by side with a real legislature; they both create a constitution far more like that of the US or the German Empire than the Constitution of modern England.

It is curious to note the analogy in some points between the Cromwellian Constitution of 1653 and one at least of the Napoleonic Constitutions. In the Acte Additional of 1815 there is an attempt to combine a strong executive under Napoleon with a real legislature.

The Emperor retains most of the powers which are given him by earlier Imperial constitutions, but he also creates a legislature and nominally concedes Ministerial responsibility. It is however to be noted that certain things, e.g. the recall of the Bourbons, the re-establishment of the feudal nobility, interferences with the rights acquired under the sale of the national domains are positively prohibited by the Constitution (art. 67).

Secondly, the Instrument of Government is a record of the opinion of the age as to the relation between the Crown and the legislature. The Puritans were in one sense rather Conservatives than innovators. The object of the Instrument of Government was to give to the one person, or Protector, the authority exercised by an ideal English monarch, e.g. Elizabeth. Hence the Constitution is to be Parliamentary in the sense that there is to be a parliament which meets at no long intervals and legislates. The government is to be according to law; the Government, further, is to be carried on by a Council just as the old Tudor administration was carried on by the Privy Council. But while Parliament is to be a regular part of the Constitution there is no intention of subordinating the Protector especially when acting with the concurrence of his Council, or to use the old formula, as King in Council, to Parliament. He is to be the powerful head of a powerful Executive, and though it is hoped that the Executive and Parliament will act in harmony, it is certainly not intended that the Government shall be a Parliamentary executive like a modern Cabinet. The notion in short of the time was the same which had always prevailed in England up to that period, namely that while the head of the Government, whether King or Protector, should pay attention to the advice of the Legislature, and should legislate only in concurrence with the Legislature, yet the monarch or "one person" should be a real, independent power, or, to use modern phraseology, a non-parliamentary executive. This, be it added, was the idea both of William III and Anne. It could not be carried out by the two first Georges, but it was within certain limits revived by George III. As already pointed out there are two possible conceptions of Parliamentary government. According to the one conception the executive and the legislature each exercise a real and independent power, though when the head of the executive is wise and the legislature patriotic they ought each to act together. This conception which involves the existence of an extra parliamentary executive, prevailed in England in the 17th century and was not entirely expelled by the other view until at any rate the accession of the House of Hanover.

According to the rival conception which now prevails in England, the legislature indirectly appoints, controls and dismisses the executive body. This view when fully developed leads inevitably to a Parliamentary executive, whereof the now prevalent form is a "Cabinet" chosen by the Legislature from among its members. This is in essence the form of government existing in England, in the British colonies, in France and in various constitutional Kingdoms.

Englishmen find it difficult to understand the position of a legislature or Parliament which does not appoint or control the executive government. A legislature, they assume, must either be powerless or in reality all powerful. A parliament which bona fide does not appoint the government must, they fancy, be like the Assemblies of the first French Empire really subordinate to the executive even in matters of legislation and be no better therefore than a sham legislative body. A legislature on the other hand which has bona fide legislative authority must, they conceive, be or soon become like the English Parliament the controller and elector of the government.

This view rests in the main on the supposed lessons of English history, but it is sometimes supported by a line of *a priori* reasoning which may be thus summed up: a Parliament, it is argued, which has real power to make laws, must gain control of the Executive; for the government is bound to obey the laws made by the legislature and Parliament may always indirectly use its legislative authority so as to curtail the power of action and therefore ultimately to control the policy of the Government.

The doctrine however that a legislature cannot possess real power of law making without becoming all powerful or sovereign is, though plausible, erroneous.

Its unsoundness is shewn by experience. The President of the US cannot control the legislative authority of Congress, nor can the Houses of Congress control except to a very limited degree the President's choice of his Ministers, or the President's action as head of the Government. No vote of the Houses could have prevented President Lincoln from surrendering to England the Confederate envoys taken from the Trent. It would have been impossible for the Houses to dictate either directly or indirectly the terms in which President Cleveland should refer in his Message to the question of free trade. No doubt the party by whom an American president is elected can exert influence over his policy; the Senate can refuse Senatorial approval to some of his appointments. But the influence of partisans is not the same thing as interference by the legislature and the Senate's opportunity of imposing a veto upon appointments arises from the Senate possessing under the Constitution a certain amount of Executive authority. Nor does English history support the notion that a Parliament if not powerless must of necessity become supreme. Under the Tudors, under Charles II, under William and under Anne, Parliament was a real legislature. No laws could be passed which were not sanctioned by Parliamentary authority. But under none of these monarchs was the Government a really Parliamentary Executive. A singular but most instructive example of the possible separation between legislative and executive power is found in the annals of Ireland during the existence of what is called Grattan's[76] Constitution, i.e. between 1782 and 1800. The Irish Parliament was the only legislature which existed in Ireland. No man Tory or Whig denied its absolute and exclusive authority to legislate for Ireland, but the Parliament which could legislate could not either in theory or in fact control or appoint the executive. In modern Germany we see the same phenomenon. The Diet is a true Imperial legislature, the Emperor cannot pass laws without the Diet's assent, but the federal parliament which can reject Bismarck's[77] proposed legislation could neither remove Bismarck from office nor, were Bismarck dismissed by the Emperor, reinstate him in power.

Nor let anyone have recourse to the empty form of words that the doctrine of the necessary supremacy of any real legislature is unsound in practice but true in theory. The *a priori* argument by which it is maintained is unsound. The contention that a true legislature can always make itself supreme over the Executive rests on the assumption that a legislative body may not possess equally with an Executive a real though limited power and this again rests on the further assumption that it is impossible for two authorities in the same State to be each supreme in a different sphere. Such supremacy depends at bottom on the capacity of each authority to command popular obedience and those who maintain the necessary supremacy

76 [Henry Grattan, (1746–1820), a leading spokesman of the Irish nationalist agitation. – Ed.]

77 [Otto von Bismarck (1815–98), prime minister of Prussia, 1862–73, 1873–90; first chancellor of the German Empire, 1871–90. – Ed.]

of a real legislature in reality contend that in a conflict between the legislature and the Executive the people or the mass of them will always obey either the one or the other and that one which commands obedience is in reality supreme or sovereign. This dogma rests on no satisfactory basis for it does not allow of the possibility or probability of the people rendering obedience to the legislature on one class of subjects and to the Executive on another. The citizens that is to say, believe in and wish for the division of powers and as long as this is the sentiment of the nation this division of powers will, whether prescribed by the constitution or merely upheld by custom, in general exist. Whether, if the legislature or the Executive encroach upon the sphere of the other, the encroachment will receive popular support is a question which admits not of an *a priori* answer; the contest beginning in 1862 and lasting till 1866 between Bismarck and the Prussian Parliament ended in a drawn battle. Whatever may be the verdict of a constitutionalist on the point of law at issue between the Minister and the Parliamentary majority, a philosophic historian will without difficulty perceive the true lesson of the struggle. The Prussian people wished for a Parliamentary government, they did not wish to be governed by Parliament. Their ideal was the rule of a strong King co-existing with the authority of a real legislature. The King was to reign and the legislature was to make laws. This ideal which was also that of English Parliamentarians down to 1689 and to a certain extent of American Republicans in 1789 found its realisation first in Prussia and then in the German Empire.

The dogma that a real legislature of necessity controls the executive can be established neither by experience nor by theory. A fact however of great importance is often confounded with the doctrine of Parliamentary supremacy. This fact is that an executive which consists of members of the legislature or which is called upon to explain or defend its action before the legislature is apt to become more or less under legislative control and therefore under whatever form to turn into a Parliamentary Executive.

Hence under most Constitutions framed with a view to maintain the separation of powers the rule has generally been laid down that the members of the Government shall not be members of the legislature. This is the principle rigorously maintained in the US. It has been embodied in many French Constitutions, as for example the monarchical constitution of 1791, the Directorial Constitution of 1795, the Consular Constitution of 1799, the various succeeding Imperial Constitutions down to 1814 and the revived Imperial constitution of 1852. Note further that with a view to maintain the independence of the Executive Ministers have under many of these Constitutions been unable to take part in the debates of the legislative assemblies. Experience shows that both these precautions are if not necessary at any rate highly expedient for the maintenance of an extra-parliamentary government when Ministers can be appointed from among the members of Parliament it is hardly possible without a direct quarrel with the legislature to maintain a Ministry not consisting of Parliamentary notabilities. A Government again which must defend its acts in Parliamentary debate is apt to become far more rapidly than could *a priori* have been expected amenable to the sentiment of Parliament. A singular example of this tendency is to be found in the later history of the second French Empire. The Opposition was at no time formidable in numbers, yet a very small body of hostile critics made their influence felt in the Imperial legislature from the moment that Ministers were allowed to take part in debate and were forced either to endure in silence, or to answer in argument the criticism of opponents. Men are at least so far rational that when once debate is opened they feel it almost intolerable to admit that their acts cannot be defended by reasoning. The experience of Ireland during the 18th century tells in the same direction. That Parliament possessed limited legislative authority and no executive power, yet its debates influenced the opinion of the country and the action of Government.

B. Comparative merits of Parliamentary Executives and of extra-parliamentary Executives

A parliamentary executive possesses at least four great merits.

1. Its connection with Parliament obviates or tends to obviate conflicts between the legislature and the Government:

When an Assembly dismisses controls and appoints the Executive it is all but impossible that there should be any lengthy conflict between the legislature and the government. Such contests have no doubt occasionally arisen in England, but the reason of this is that the cabinet has been or is to be a limited extent appointed by authorities outside the legislature and has not been or is not, a thoroughly Parliamentary executive. The greater the control of Parliament the less the chance of conflicts between Parliament and Cabinet.

A contest is an undoubted evil. It always produces a waste of national strength; it may produce danger of revolution. President Johnson's[78] disagreement with Congress involved the US in new risks of commotion and it is quite possible lost to the nation some of the advantages gained by the war against Secession. The conflict and intrigues which characterised the presidency of Louis Napoleon were terminated only by the *Coup d'etat*.

2. Cabinet government which is the best developed form of a Parliamentary executive immensely facilitates the easy transaction of business. The contrast drawn on this point by Bagehot[79] between the procedure of Congress and the procedure of the English Parliament, confirmed as it is in every respect by Mr Bryce, is decisive.

3. Cabinet government leads to the selection for executive functions of men whose character is personally known to the electors, i.e. the House,

78 [Andrew Johnson (1808–75), president of the US, 1865–9. – Ed.]

79 [Walter Bagehot (1826–77), political commentator, economist; famous work: *The English Constitution* (1867). – Ed.]

by whom they are appointed. The House of Commons know as a body the qualities good or bad of Lord Salisbury or Mr Gladstone, of Lord Hartington[80] or of Sir William Harcourt[81] in a way in which these qualities cannot possibly be known to outsiders. Cabinet government again puts or ought to put in power, men who have gained reputation in Parliament and through their Parliamentary reputation are known to the nation. Cabinet government means or ought to mean government by known statesmen. It is hardly conceivable that a man should become Prime Minister in England whose name and antecedents were unknown to the English people. Lord Bute[82] was hardly known to an English elector till George III created him to the most unpopular of England's Premiers. When Mr Polk[83] was installed in office as President of the US a man in the crowd shouted "who is Mr Polk?" and the question elicited roars of sympathetic laughter. The tendency of Cabinet government to place known men in power is probably its greatest recommendation; unfortunately since the day when Bagehot wrote his defence or eulogy of this system of administration experience has taught us that Cabinet government need not of necessity mean the rule of notable persons. Of the constantly changing French Ministries few persons outside France know the names. Frenchmen themselves, it is said, often know little of the Ministers who hold office. The most noticeable fact of modern French politics is that the best known among Republican statesmen is banished from Parliament and is said to be permanently excluded from office.

4. Cabinet government facilitates a change in the system of administration:

A minister is in power well suited for the conduct of home affairs; he is a man of peace and has come into office during a period of general

80 [Lord Hartington (1833–1908), leader of the Liberal Unionist Party, opposed Gladstone's Irish Home Rule. – Ed.]

81 [Sir William Harcourt (1827–1904), home secretary, 1880–5, chancellor of the exchequer, 1886, 1892–4. – Ed.]

82 [Lord John Bute (1713–92), first lord of the treasury, 1762–3. – Ed.]

83 [James Polk (1795–1849), president of the US, 1845–9. –Ed.]

tranquillity. A war or a rebellion breaks out. Everyone feels that the pacific Premier is not the man for the time. He can at once be changed by a vote of the House of Commons and the man whom the nation deem most suited for the emergency be put in his place. All that can be said on this advantage of Cabinet government has been said so well by Mr Bagehot that it were useless to repeat and impertinent to alter what he has written. The defects of Cabinet government are so to speak the seamy sides of its merits.

i. Legislation is hopelessly mixed up with the question of a Ministry's tenure of power. Laws in the English Parliament are never discussed on their own merits. As further office depends upon success in administration, all who wish to gain office, in other words the opposition, try to make the administration of the Government end in failure. The administration of the government is however nothing but the management of national affairs. The object therefore of every Opposition is more or less consciously to prevent the successful management of national business. This need not argue want of patriotism. If A's accession to power and the success of the political principles which A advocates depends upon showing that B's management of public business is a succession of blunders, the best known laws of human nature make it a certainty that A will bona fide think B a disastrous blunderer.

ii. Cabinet government means government which because it is easily changed is apt to become changeable. The success of a policy depends upon a series of accidents; a Ministry dare not be even for a moment unpopular and a Ministry which never dare be unpopular cannot always follow its own ideas of wisdom.

Turn now to the characteristics of an extra-parliamentary Executive. Its demerits are a constantly recurring and dangerous tendency to conflicts with the legislature. A great want of pliability in the transaction of any affairs wherein cooperation between the legislature and the executive is desirable and lastly the possibility of its producing the rule of an unknown man.

This last is probably the worst of the evil results which may fairly be attributed to the existence of an executive not under the control of the legislature. If the real head of the government be an hereditary monarch then at any moment the holder of supreme authority may be a man whose qualities are either unfitted for government or quite unknown to people he is going to govern. Frederick the Great when he came to the throne was thought a sentimentalist. Few are the persons who can pronounce decisively on the talents and disposition of the German Emperor or the Russian Czar. If he be appointed by popular election the apparent securities for his being either known or capable are on the whole illusory. "I should be a good president", said an American, "but I would be the worst of candidates for the Presidency". Louis Napoleon was elected by 5 millions of votes at a time when not one Frenchmen in 10 thousand knew whether Louis Napoleon was a fool or a genius.

An extra-parliamentary executive possessed or may possess, two merits.

First – questions of legislation may under such a government be to a certain extent separated from questions of administration. Where the rejection or passing of a bill does not involve the existence of a Ministry, bills may possibly be discussed on their own merits.

Secondly – An extra-parliamentary executive, such for example as that planned by Cromwell, ought to be far more independent than a parliamentary Cabinet of temporary terms of popular opinion. A man whether Emperor, Protector, or President who knows that a blunder or the appearance of a blunder will not entail a fall from power may especially in administrative matters do what seems to him best or most just independently of the popularity of his acts. No one can doubt that Cromwell and Lincoln were each able to act with an independence of immediate popularity which is all but forbidden to any modern Premier.

C. Comparison between the Constitution of 1653 & the Modern Constitution of England

Did the first Protectorate really resemble the modern constitutional monarchy of England?

A student's first impulse is to answer this question in the affirmative.

The constitutionalist of 1653, as represented by the Instrument of Government were both innovators & democrats. They advanced in some respects very far towards the realisation of modern ideas. Under their hands Parliament became a regular & normal part of the Constitution. Parliament itself was reformed & reformed much upon the lines which were tardily followed in 1832 & since 1832 under the Commonwealth was for the first time united every part of what now forms the United Kingdom & for the first time England was provided with a strong regular army & with a sufficient navy. Add to all this that in theory at least the doctrines of toleration were more distinctly recognized as a part of the law of the land than they have ever been recognized in England until quite modern times & whatever may be said as to the restrictions placed upon the operation of this theory, no fair critic can doubt that had the Constitution of 1653 endured all orthodox Protestants would have enjoyed practical toleration & what many of them did not enjoy till more than a century after the revolution of 1689, political equality. It must never be forgotten that in point of toleration Cromwell & his followers were far in advance of their age.

But a little reflection will make us feel that though the Constitution of the Protectorate was in theory at least a democratic constitution & in more respects than one carried out ideas which were now associate with freedom & progress yet the constitutionalism of 1653 was not only accidently but essentially different from the English Constitutionalism of 1897. It is of some importance to seize this fundamental dissimilarity. Had the Constitution of 1653 stood England might have been a perfectly free country & would have been a country possessing Parliamentary institutions. But the Republican Constitution of England would have been something very different from the existing constitutional monarchy. The mere fact indeed that the Protectorate was under the Constitution of 1653 not hereditary is a comparatively small matter. The main importance of the office of Protector being elective lies in the weight thereby given to the Council as electors of each successive Protector. The points which are really worth notice are these: The Constitution of England was turned into a written & rigid constitution. A strong Executive was erected armed with powers greater than have been ever held by any English King. In the Council was formed a body which might in all matters of administration have overbalanced the power of the legislature. It might very probably have become cooptative. Parliament, lastly, was transformed into a merely legislative body, it did not in reality appoint the Executive nor did it retain the powers by which Parliament has indirectly gained a right to nominate or at any rate to control the nomination of the executive body. Cromwell & the men who drew up the Instrument of 1653 might be called in one sense democrats, though the term does not very happily describe them. They were not parliamentarians; they wished to make Parliament a part but not the predominant part of the Constitution; they, whether knowingly or not, created a Parliament with restricted powers which should legislate but should not govern. Their constitutionalism has some points of affinity with the constitutionalism of the United States. It has yet stronger points of likeness to the constitutionalism of Germany. It does not in its essential characteristics resemble the parliamentary constitutionalism of modern England. Paradoxical though the assertion sound, the Cromwellian ideal of government had a good deal more affinity to the ideal of Strafford or of Bismarck than it has to the ideal represented in the world of politics by Pitt, or Peel, or Gladstone, or in the world of literature by Hallam[84] and Macaulay.[85]

84 [Henry Hallam (1777–1859) published his classic *The Constitutional History of England, from the Accession of Henry VII to the Death of George II* in 1827. – Ed.]

85 [Thomas Babington Macaulay wrote a long review of Hallam's *Constitutional History of England* in September 1828. See T.B. Macaulay, *Critical Historical Essays* (London, 1850). – Ed.]

5

English Constitutionalism under George the Third (1785)

[No date]

A. Outward Likeness to modern constitutionalism[86]

1. Forms similar
2. Government Parliamentary in full sense
3. Government national
4. Absence of arbitrary power

B. Differences from modern constitutionalism

I. Differences in form of Constitution

   1. Parliament a *British* Parliament
   2. Parliament a *Protestant* Parliament and (practically) a Church of England Parliament
   3. Parliament an *unreformed* Parliament

86 See generally Paley, *op. cit.*, Book VI, ch. vii; E. Boutmy, *Etudes de Droit Constitionnel: France–Angleterre–Etats Unis* (Paris, 1885).

II. Differences in *working* of institutions
1. The influence of the Crown
2. The influence of the Aristocracy
3. The position of the Cabinet

III. Differences in *spirit* of the Constitution
1. Form of Constitution practically unchangeable
2. Constitution rested on predominance of certain classes
3. Constitution neither in theory nor in practice democratic
4. Executive supported by Crown had considerable independence
5. Independence of Parliament
6. Limited sphere of States activity

Whoever compares the constitutionalism of Queen Victoria with the constitutionalism of the Commonwealth feels himself, so to speak, in a strange country. The more he considers the matter the more he is struck with the essential differences between the political ideas of the Puritans & the political ideas of today. Cromwell, it is true, wished like every other Puritan statesman to establish the rule of law & of freedom. His constant endeavour was to rule not without, but with a Parliament. He had no wish to be a despot. But he was utterly unfitted for the part of a constitutional King. He could far more easily have been an American President, such as Jackson[87] or Lincoln, or a modern German Emperor such as was William I, or such as aspires to be his grandson. His Council was utterly unlike a modern Cabinet; one is forced to compare it not with an English Ministry but with the American Senate, not indeed as the Senate now is, but such as it was designed to be by the founders of the United States. Parliament again,

87 [Andrew Jackson (1767–1845), president of the US, 1829–37. – Ed.]

as constituted by the Instrument of Government is in its whole character a very different thing from any Parliament which has sat in England since the Revolution of 1689. It consists of one House, it has for many purposes uncontrolled powers of legislation; it had little hold on the Executive. The Commonwealth, it may be said, was a Democracy, & so also is the constitutional Monarchy of Victoria. This remark is true but misleading. The Commonwealth was always in fact a Government supported by a mere fraction of the people & the Democracy on which, had it lasted, it must ultimately have rested, was a Democracy of independent landowners & under the Instrument of Government a Democracy of comparatively well to do landowners. The constitutional Monarchy is now supported by the whole nation; the government is in reality democratic but the democracy by which it is upheld is in the main a democracy of townsfolk. The majority of the electors are tradesmen, artisans & labourers. The truth is that, as already pointed out, our Puritan forefathers aimed at results such as freedom from arbitrary power, the establishment of civil liberty, & to a certain extent of religious toleration which their descendants have obtained. But the path by which these results were reached is not the path marked out by the Whigs of 1689 & followed out in ways which the Whigs of 1689 never foresaw, by the Liberals & reformers of later days. The ideas of the Commonwealth have either not been developed at all or have received their full development rather in the United States than in England. It were indeed an error to suppose that the great Rebellion left no permanent traces on the institutions of England, but it is true that the Interregnum constitutes a break in the development of the English Constitution. The ideas, no less than the institutions of the Commonwealth, though they constitute a premature attempt to realise some essentially modern & democratic conceptions cannot be made to square with the modern conceptions of constitutional government. It is at bottom the differences between the constitutionalism of the 17th & the constitutionalism of the 19th century which impresses any one who takes in hand the comparative study of institutions.

A critic, on the other hand, who compares the Constitution as it existed in the reign of George III, say in 1787 [*sic*], with the Constitution as it now exists in 1897 is in danger of exaggerating the points of likeness & overlooking some important, though less marked, points of dissimilarity. In 1787 the forms of the Constitution were much what they are at present. The King was strictly a constitutional Monarch; there existed a regular Cabinet supported by the majority of the House of Commons & the Cabinet was under the leadership of an acknowledged Premier. Pitt was as much a Prime Minister & the head of the Government (though neither he nor his contemporaries would have called the Government Pitt's Government) as Mr Gladstone or Lord Salisbury. It was fully understood that the House of Commons was the predominant body in the State, & it had come to be acknowledged that a majority of the House could not long retain its power unless it were supported by a majority of the electorate. George the Third, though a man who passionately loved power, never affected to be in any sense above the law. He never ruled or conceived it possible to rule, without a Parliament; he never claimed to create a Parliamentary borough; he never made use of the Royal Veto; he was perfectly aware that he must always act through Ministers & that no Minister could long keep office who could not command the votes of the House of Commons. Both in form & in fact Parliamentary government was established in England & the unbroken continuity of our constitutional development tempts a student to think that the constitutionalism of George III was in all material matters the constitutionalism of today. Yet any one who looks a little below the surface will feel that here, as elsewhere, continuity is a totally different thing from identity & that both in form & still more in spirit, the Georgian differed from the Victorian Constitution. Our aim should be to make perfectly clear to ourselves what are the points of real similarity, or even identity & also of important difference.

A. The points of likeness

The essential point of likeness, we might even say of identity, is that by 1787, & indeed from the accession of the Hanoverian dynasty, the Monarchy had become in the strict sense both constitutional & Parliamentary. This was the work of the Whigs; it resulted both from the Revolution of 1689 & from the maintenance on the throne of the House of Hanover. Till 1745 the possibility of another Restoration made it necessary for the Hanoverian Kings, though both of them by nature despotic enough, to respect the Constitution & to maintain parliamentary government. By the time George III ascended the throne the authority of Parliament had been established past dispute. The constitutional government of George III differed greatly from the constitutional government of Victoria but it belonged at bottom to the same class of governments. Each as fully acknowledged the rule of law, under each form of government Parliament & above all the House of Commons, has become the most important body in the country.

It is worth while to work out this fundamental similarity a little more into detail & note the main features which the English Constitution of 1787 has in common with the Constitution of 1897.

Arbitrary power is quite unknown. Under George III the law of the land was in many respects harsh & severe. The frequency of capital punishment & of even more frequent condemnations to death for very slight offences, & the constant imprisonment of debtors are two examples whereof scores might be found of the prevalence of a spirit of severity or of cruelty unknown to the present day; but though the law might be cruel every man was subject to the law & to the law alone & no man stood in danger of losing life, liberty or property, simply because he opposed the will of the King.

The annual meeting of Parliament, though not directly guaranteed by any law was as much part of the Constitution as it is now. It had become, so to speak, a political law of nature, & all opposition between Crown &

Parliament had come to an end. George III exerted, it is true, very considerable authority. By means of what was called influence he could when he chose influence the action of the House of Commons but he never in reality came into conflict with Parliament. On one celebrated occasion he systematically defied a Parliamentary majority, but he ventured upon this course because he, or rather Pitt, had the sagacity to perceive that the House did not represent the electors & that a dissolution would produce a House of Commons ready to support the policy of the King.

In the earlier part of his career George had struggled against the growth of Cabinet government as we now understand it. He knew that he could act only through Ministers; he knew that his Ministers must command Parliamentary support, but he contended for the right to exercise a very wide discretion in the choice of his servants. He wished probably not to have an acknowledged Premier & rather to act through Ministers each of whom should be the head of a particular Department, than through a collective Ministry or Cabinet. But before George III came to the throne the possibility of permanently resisting the possibility of Cabinet government had passed away, for the rule was established that the King was not present at the meetings of the Cabinet. By 1787 the King had, though perhaps he was hardly conscious of the fact, given up in substance, though not in form, the effort to oppose the growth of a Parliamentary Executive. A conflict of more than 20 years ended, as have so many constitutional conflicts in England in a very singular compromise. The King defeated the political party which he most detested, & overthrew the Government which had been forced upon him by an overwhelming Parliamentary majority. He appointed a Premier of his own choice, but Pitt whom he chose was supported from the first not only by the King but by the nation. The temporary defeat of an artificial majority constituted by an unprincipled coalition of factions procured for the King a striking triumph, but the triumph was purchased by his admitting in effect the sovereignty of the nation.

By 1787, & indeed long before that date, the supremacy of the nation had in effect become an essential part of the Constitution. George III made many mistakes, one or two of which inflicted incalculable damage on the country, & as they were denounced by the most prudent statesmen & the ablest thinkers of the time, might have been avoided by a King of genius or enlightenment. But the plain truth is that George's worst errors were sanctioned, if not applauded by his people. The policy of England was in the long run the policy approved by Englishmen. "The present representation", says Paley, after dwelling on its obvious defects, "is still in such a degree popular, or rather the representatives are so connected with the mass of the community by a society of interests and passions, that the will of the people, when it is determined, permanent, & general, almost always at length prevails".[88]

B. The points of difference

In spite of outward resemblances the Georgian Constitution is distinguished from the modern Constitution of England by differences in its form, in its working, in its spirit.[89]

88 Paley, *op. cit.*, Book VI, ch. vii, p. 490.

89 The best authority for the character of the Georgian Constitution is Paley, *op. cit.*, Book VI, ch. vii. The book is the work of a man who looked at the Constitution as it actually existed. He has seen it & described it far more truly than either Burke, who was led astray by his rhetoric & his imagination, & Blackstone, who though a writer of supreme literary gift, either mistook forms for realities or did not care to distinguish them. The importance of the book as a picture of the Constitution is increased by the date of its publication. It appeared in 1785. At that moment the modern Cabinet system was firmly established under Pitt & men's views of the Constitution were not yet biassed [*sic*] by either enthusiasm for, or detestation of the French Revolution.

Differences in form

1. The Parliament of George III was in 1785 the Parliament of Great Britain & not the Parliament of the United Kingdom. It was a British, we might say an English Parliament. It was not what our present Parliament is, an Anglo-Irish Parliament.

This point, though obvious, has great importance. Up till the beginning of this century not a single member from Ireland sat in the Parliament at Westminster. Strictly Irish affairs did not occupy Parliament after 1782 at all. The Scotch members moreover were only 45 in a House of Commons consisting of 548 members. To put the matter broadly only a twelfth part of the House was Scotch. The rest were wholly English. The Scotch members acted, we may be pretty sure, together. They had practically a decisive voice on purely Scotch affairs. The chief effect of their presence as regards English policy was to strengthen the administration of the day or rather the Crown. On all English matters, on all matters of general policy England was during the 18th century governed by Englishmen in accordance with English ideas.

2. The Parliament was strictly a Protestant Parliament & though not absolutely yet with very slight limitations a Church of England Parliament.

No Roman Catholic could by any possibility occupy a seat either in the House of Commons or in the House Lords & no Roman Catholic could vote at an election. Roman Catholics in fact were excluded from the public life of England & even had they been admitted to the franchise & to seats in Parliament they could up to 1800 have exercised no substantial influence on English public life. They were not in England practically persecuted or even disliked by the educated classes though Papists were, as witness the Gordon Riots[90] of 1780, hateful to the mob. Their numbers were very small.

90 [Lord George Gordon (1751–93), supported by a large group of Protestants led a march to Westminster against the Government's Catholic Relief Act of 1778. Violence followed, which left over 300 dead. – Ed.]

The Catholic gentry represented a dying class, so to speak. There were no Irish constituencies to send to England Roman Catholic representatives, & there was, I conceive, no extensive Irish emigration to fill the large towns with Irish labourers or artisans, & if the Irish poor had already settled in England they would not for the most part have obtained votes. Growing towns, such as Birmingham or Manchester, were unrepresented & though in one or two constituencies there existed a wide franchise approaching to universal suffrage, in most boroughs a resident working man, whether Irishman or Englishman, had no vote at all. The Parliament therefore was an English Parliament dominated by English Churchmen.

3. The Parliament was an unreformed Parliament. The Parliamentary reforms introduced under the Commonwealth had historically no effect whatever. The old distribution of seats & the old franchises reappeared as a matter of course at the Restoration, & the protest of the House of Commons against the creation of a new Parliamentary borough (Newark) by Charles II practically abolished the Royal Prerogative of creating boroughs & made the gradual extension of the Parliamentary franchise to the growing cities of the North impossible.[91]

Men are still living who remember, & at least one eminent man is living, who sat in the unreformed Parliament, yet Englishmen of today do not easily realise what the Unreformed Parliament really was, or rather perhaps what it appeared to be. It looked at least like the strangest system of representation or misrepresentation under which a great nation ever enjoyed freedom & prosperity. It is easy enough if you search the right books, to find queer stories about the rotten boroughs. One of them consisted it is said of nothing but a field enclosed in a landowner's domain. The two or it might be three electors met there to elect at the landowner's direction, a member of Parliament. The true elector had marked the spot with a stone

91 The constitutional changes of the Commonwealth seem to have been absolutely forgotten.

on which was inscribed *vox populi vox Dei.* When the Reform Bill was brought forward the representative of Ludgershall delivered this speech in the House of Commons: "I am the patron of Ludgershall. I am the elector of Ludgershall. I am the member for Ludgershall. As patron, as elector, & as member, I shall vote for the abolition of Ludgershall". In Mr Walpole's painstaking or to use an old expression, painful *History of England*, may be found elaborately collected together examples of all the anomalies which were so common that the word anomalies is hardly appropriate existing under the Parliamentary system before 1832. "The 45 Scotch members", he writes, "were nominated by 35 persons. 354 members were returned on the recommendation of the Treasury, & 197 patrons. The Union with Ireland added 100 members to the roll of the House of Commons. But 51 of these were returned by 36 Peers & 20 by 19 Commoners. The Union had increased the roll of the House to 658, and 424 of the 658 members were returned either on the nomination or on the recommendation of 252 patrons". But though there is no reason whatever to doubt the accuracy of Mr Walpole's figures, the picture of a past state of things drawn, it may be, by a censorious critic, never equals in value the calm representation of an unbiassed [*sic*] contemporary. The best & shortest account known to me of the Unreformed House of Commons is given by Paley. "There is nothing in the British Constitution", he writes, "so remarkable, as the irregularity of the popular representation. The House of Commons consists of five hundred and forty-eight members, of whom two hundred are elected by seven thousand constituents; so that a majority of these seven thousand, without any reasonable title to superior weight or influence in the state, may, under certain circumstances, decide a question against the opinion of as many millions. Or to place the same object in another point of view; if my estate be situated in one county of the Kingdom, I possess the ten thousandth part of a single representative; if in another, the thousandth; if in a particular district, I may be one in twenty who choose two representatives; if in a still more favoured spot, I may enjoy the right of appointing two myself. If I have been born, or dwell, or have served an apprenticeship in one town, I am represented in the national assembly by two deputies, in the choice of whom I exercise an actual & sensible share of power; if accident has thrown my birth, or habitation, or service into another town, I have no representative at all, nor more power or concern in the election of those who make the laws by which I am governed, than if I was a subject of the Grand Signior – and this partiality subsists without any pretence whatever of merit or of propriety, to justify the preference of one place to another. Or, thirdly, to describe the state of national representation as it exists, in reality, it may be affirmed, I believe, with truth, that about one half of the House of Commons obtain their seats in that assembly by the election of the people, the other half by purchase, or by the nomination of single proprietors of great estates".[92]

So much for the difference in form between the Constitution of 1787 and the Constitution of 1897. The Constitution of 1787 may be summed up in the character of its Parliament, and that Parliament was what our present Parliament is not a substantially *English* Parliament, a *Protestant* Parliament and, lastly a Parliament specially representing the *property*, & especially the landholding classes.

Differences in the working of the Constitution

The Position of the Crown

The formal prerogatives of Queen Victoria are pretty nearly the same as the formal prerogatives of George III, but the *position* of the Crown is very different today from its position when George III was King.

92 Paley, *op. cit.*, Book VI, ch. vii, pp. 485–86.

The King possessed great & often decisive power in the government of the State. Or at least three great occasions the will of George III determined the policy of the country. This power arose partly from his character but it was due in the main to a more obvious & material cause. The Crown in 1787 controlled or influenced the House of Commons by means of what was then technically known as "influence", or, in other words, of patronage & the power of thus directing the action of Parliament arose from the fact that the Crown had at its disposal a vast amount of patronage in the way of seats in Parliament, of lucrative places, of pensions, of titles, & the like. That the amount of this influence was large & that its effects were important was admitted by all men. The evils of influence were denounced by Burke in language which no one can forget in his speech on economical reform, whilst the possible or hypothetical good effects of influence are suggested by Paley in the most ingenious of paradoxes or apologies. But neither the assailants nor the defenders of Royal influence denied its existence.

But the two points which deserve our notice are first that influence in the sense in which it existed under George III does not exist under Victoria, & secondly, that influence produced several indirect but very important effects on the working of the Georgian Constitution.

Influence no longer exists

The Government of course has places & titles at its disposal & their distribution by the Ministry of the day is a matter of great public importance, but the number of places which a Premier can freely give away are small; few of them are sinecures. He has no seats whatever by which he can at his own will introduce into or keep his followers in Parliament. Of pensions or sinecures to be given away at the will of the Crown or Ministry there are practically none. The gifts which a political leader can make to his partisans are in fact so small that they cannot by any possibility purchase a majority in the House of Commons, or even retain the allegiance of a wavering party.[93]

The existence of influence had several important results

In the first place it manifestly increased the power & authority of the Government. It counteracted the tendency which in modern political slang is called the swing of the pendulum. It prevented a Ministry from losing power simply because it had been for a long time in office & having of necessity fallen into mistakes & made faces found itself the object of increased hostility on the part of its opponents without having been able to return what may be called the personal allegiance of its friends. In estimating the effect of influence in counteracting the effect of growing unpopularity we must remember that the Crown or the Ministry possessed a number of seats which were strictly at the disposal of the Government or had in effect the power to nominate a number of M.Ps. Under George III it was a distinct & a calculable advantage for a party to be in office during a general election. At the present day it has often been maintained that at a general election the party in opposition has a slight advantage over its opponents. Influence moreover very directly, at any rate in the case of a strong man like George III, increased the personal authority of the King. He was after all,

93 Let no one however suppose that corruption is dead. It is an evil which like sin itself, will never die. It is at least judging from experience, or from our knowledge of human nature, as likely to flourish under a democratic as under an aristocratic form of government. The American Congress is at least as, & the legislature of New York far more corrupt than ever was the worst House of Commons. It is further as easy to corrupt classes as individuals. All that is maintained in the text is that corruption in the present day cannot exist in the form of influence of the Crown. Paley & no doubt other acute observers, perceived that reform of Parliament would mean the abolition of influence.

in theory the man who appointed to every public office: he was the great patron & George was determined that his patronage should be under his control. For a certain period he made himself in virtue of his influence the real head of the State. It was the King, & not Lord North[94], who from 1770 to 1782 guided the policy of the country. The calamities of the war with the Colonies made it impossible for the King to retain the power he had acquired, but thus much he finally established; that influence should be exercised either by the King or by a Minister whom he cordially supported. As long as George III maintained his throne & his sanity the Crown was a most important factor, if not the most important factor in the working of the Constitution. Two facts give us some measure of the power possessed by the Crown. In 1788 Pitt was the most popular of Premiers, yet every one expected that if the Prince of Wales became Regent, Pitt would be turned out of office & the Whigs placed in power. Whether the result would have followed may be doubtful, but it is certain that popular opinion attributed even to a Regent, & to a Regent whose moral character would have carried no weight, the power to determine who should be Prime Minister. There cannot be a doubt, again, that between 1801 & 1804 the country desired to put Pitt in power. Yet Addington[95] was kept in office & the members of Parliament prepared to follow Pitt in opposition to the Government were apparently small.

In the second place the existence of influence, combined no doubt with other circumstances, made politics in the last century a professional career.

If we want to have a notion of change in this matter which has taken place in recent times, we should note two facts. The one is that the lower class of politicians, the Rigbys[96] of the day, certainly made & intended to

94 [Lord Frederick North (1732–92), prime minister, 1770–82. – Ed.]
95 [Lord Henry Addington (1757–1844), prime minister, 1801–4. – Ed.]
96 [Sir John Rigby (1834–1903), judge, liberal politician. – Ed.]

make a gain out of politics. Theodore Hook,[97] who could be described as little better than a political satirist of a low type received a place in Jamaica it is true, of £2000 a year. Pitt was admittedly in pecuniary matters the most disinterested of men, but Pitt who is said to have had about £300 a year of his own received for the greater part of his life an income of some £ 10.000 a year & as Warden of Walmer Castle, held, what was equivalent to a good pension on retirement. Burke, again, was in some respects the noblest statesman of his time, yet Burke who was the son of an Irish attorney & who at the early part of his career edited the Annual Register it is said for £100 a year, & who most nobly gave up for the sake of his political convictions the chances or certainty of holding gainful offices which fell to men who gained the favour of the Crown did nevertheless in some form or other make a livelihood out of politics. He received £ 30.000 from Lord Rockingham, he purchased a landed estate, at the end of his life he received a handsome but well deserved pension from the Crown & and is said to have been at his death on the point of receiving a Peerage. These things are not of course mentioned as charges against men of extraordinary genius & of the highest integrity. They are referred to as showing that a century ago political life was a profession just as legal life is a profession at the present day. The blanks no doubt were in the field of politics as now in the field of law, far more numerous than the prizes. Still the prizes were great & relatively more valuable than we now imagine. The mercantile millionaires of the 19th century were unknown & the gains of authors were trifling. Professional fees were as measured by our standard, small. Politics in short was to those who ventured on the hazardous pursuit a profession like any other. It is a profession no longer. The politician who has made a fortune in politics does not exist or, if this statement be deemed exaggerated, it is certain that no sensible man goes into politics with the idea that he will make a fortune in Parliament. Hence the 18th century presents more than one example of a character which no longer exists, viz. the patriotic adventurer. The noblest

97 [Theodore Hook (1788–1841) writer and hoaxer, editor of the *John Bull* (estab. in 1820). – Ed.]

of this class was Burke. We may call him an adventurer because he meant to make politics his profession & a profession which would support him. He entered so far into public life in the same spirit in which a man of high character, such as Roundell Palmer,[98] goes to the Bar; he intends to succeed in an honourable career by the use of honourable means, & he does so. But he conceals neither from himself nor from others that he intends also that his professional career shall provide him with a competence, &, it may be, with a fortune. We call Burke a patriot because he devoted his genius to the promotion of the public welfare, & throughout his life was ready to sacrifice his fortunes to his principles.

The Position of Peerage & House of Lords

From the accession, at any rate, of George I, the House of Commons, & not the House of Lords, was the most important body in the State. But the weight of the Peerage in England has never depended on the constitutional powers of the House of Lords. It is far nearer the truth to say that the House derives its power from the Peerage than that the Peerage derives its authority from the powers of the House. The House of Lords itself had more weight in the time of George than at the present day. On one celebrated occasion at any rate the House in effect overthrew a Ministry supported by a large majority in the Commons, but this triumph was due not to the inherent powers of the House but to the energetic support of the King & of the electors. What is more to the purpose as showing the weight of the House itself is the fact that on the whole the House under the influence of Whig magnates was more favourable to toleration than was the House of Commons. The true source of the power of the Peerage was that they were the chiefs of the class, namely the whole body of landowners who were then predominant in the State. As the century passed away the mercantile classes – a somewhat different thing from the

98 [Lord Roundell Palmer (1812–95), lord chancellor, 1872–4, 1880–5. – Ed.]

manufacturing classes – increased in power, but Pitt, whether designedly or not, freely promoted men of wealth to Peerages & the House of Lords came to represent the mercantile no less than the landed interest. The Peers moreover made up for their want of authority in their own House by the influence they exercised over the House of Commons. To them in the main belonged the nomination boroughs. A glance through Oldfield's[99] *Representative History* will easily explain the methods by which harmony was maintained between the Commons & the Lords & the power which up to the passing of the Reform Bill was exercised by the Peers.

Position of Cabinet

The Cabinets of George III were smaller than some of them not being half the size of a modern Cabinet. Pitt's first Cabinet for example, consisted of seven members. It was for purposes of government a body which under a powerful Premier might make a compact & vigorous Executive.

Differences in the spirit of the Constitution

Few things are more difficult of definition than the expression "spirit of a Constitution". It has, to say the truth, at least two or three different meanings. It may mean for example the end or final cause for which a Constitution or law, or institutions generally exist or may be supposed to exist. This is apparently the sense in which the word "spirit" is used by Montesquieu in *Esprit des Lois*. It may, again, mean something very near to the working of a Constitution, but the term refers rather to the way in which the persons of a given time look upon their institutions, the way in which they expect them to work or assume that they will work than to the actual

99 [Thomas Oldfield (1755–1822), political reformer and historian; major work: *History of the Original Constitutions of Parliaments* (1797). – Ed.]

working of the institutions themselves. The words I am going to use seem pedantic, yet they more nearly express my meaning than any others. The spirit of institutions is the subjective side of their working. When we say for instance, that the spirit of English institutions is legal, or that the spirit of Prussian institutions is military, what we really mean is that Englishmen as a rule, look at their institutions from a legal point of view, & expect that the law will be rigidly respected, & what has been termed the rule of law be maintained, whilst Prussians look upon their institutions from the point of view of soldiers, that military ideas are predominant amongst the Government & the people, that they expect that the authority of the State shall be maintained & that the Constitution shall comply with the requirements of a well & justly governed army. It must however at once be admitted that the term "spirit" is an extremely vague one, which conveys a notion as indefinite as it is important. It is certain to anyone who with adequate knowledge meditates upon the matter that the spirit of Georgian Constitutionalism was very different from the spirit of Victorian Constitutionalism. My aim is to enumerate some of the points in which this difference of spirit is apparent.

1. *The forms of the Constitution were practically unchangeable.*

The theoretical sovereignty of Parliament was at least as well established in 1787 as in 1897. The classical passage for the definition or description of Parliamentary sovereignty is to be found in Blackstone. But for all this the sovereignty of Parliament was far less a reality in the 18th than it has become towards the end of the 19th century. No one expected that any government would propose or carry fundamental changes in the political institutions of England & the expectation was fully justified by historical facts. From 1689 to 1828 there was, if we except the Acts of Union with Scotland & Ireland no fundamental change made by legal enactment in the Constitution of the country. This tacit & almost unconscious Conservatism is a marked feature of the 18th century politics. The simple truth is that among the Englishmen who cared about politics at all there existed profound & if you looked at the matter from a practical point of view, not unreasonable satisfaction with the national institutions. Political parties were divided as to the policy of the country not as to the maintenance of its institutions. The most Conservative government of modern days proposes every year changes which a century ago would have startled the most energetic of Whig reformers.

2. *The Constitution rested on the predominance of certain classes: the large landowners, the merchants, the independent freeholders, & the like.*

There was in reality though not in name, something analogous to the body which used in France to be described as the "legal country", or the limited body of citizens who, e.g. under Louis Philippe, alone exercised full political rights & were supposed to represent the sentiment & interests of the whole nation, & let it be added, that in the England of George III the legal country to a far greater extent than one would suppose did really represent the nation, or at any rate as much of the nation as felt any effective interest in public affairs. This is the strong point of the intelligent Conservatism, a totally different thing from Toryism, represented by Burke & Paley. "Let us", writes Paley, in answer to the attacks made on the anomalies of the representative system, "before we seek to obtain anything more, consider duly what we already have. We *have* a House of Commons composed of five hundred & forty eight members, in which number are found the most considerable landholders & merchants of the Kingdom; the heads of the army, the navy, & the law; the occupiers of great offices in the state; together with many private individuals, eminent by their knowledge, eloquences, or activity. Now, if the country be not safe in such hands, in whose may it confide its interests? If such a number of such men be liable to the influence of corrupt motives, what assembly of men will be secure from the same danger? Does any new scheme of representation promise to collect together more wisdom, or to produce firmer integrity? In this view of the subject, and attending not to ideas of order and proportion (of which many minds are much enamoured), but to effects alone, we may discover just excuses for those parts of the present representation, which appear to a hasty observer most exceptional and absurd".[100]

3. *The Constitution was neither in theory nor in practice democratic.*

A constitution is in its principles democratic when it recognises the voice or the consent of the majority of the citizens as the only legitimate source of authority. In this sense the Federal Constitution of the United States, all the French Republican Constitutions, & also the French Imperial Constitutions constituted by Napoleon I or Napoleon III may be called democratic.

A Constitution is in practice democratic when the policy of the State in all matters of importance whether they be domestic or foreign, is determined by the wishes, or at any rate by the supposed wishes, of the majority of the citizens.

But, neither in principle nor in fact was the will of the numerical majority of the people supreme under George III.

The whole system of Parliamentary representation which reached the height of paradox or anomaly in the case of Scotland, where the representation of a country which contained two millions of inhabitants was confined to the *tenants of the Crown* in the several counties to a corporation of *thirty-three* individuals in the City of Edinburgh and to sixty five delegates from the same number of self elected corporations of Royal Burghs – was a theoretical & practical denial of what is called the sovereignty of the people.

Nor is there any reason to suppose that the will of the majority of the inhabitants of Great Britain was in fact supreme. It is certain that the most popular Minister of his age – Chatham[101] – was kept out of office in deference to the will of the King & also to the jealousy of the nobility. It

100 Paley, *Principles of Moral & Political Philosophy*, Book VI, ch. vii, p. 488.

101 [William Pitt the elder, Earl of Chatham (1708–78), prime minister, 1756–61, 1766–68. – Ed.]

is probable too that in some respects the actual government of the country was more "liberal" to use a modern expression, than were the opinions or prejudices of the people. English sentiment disapproved of the favour shown by George III to the Scotch, though his partiality for Scotchmen cemented the Union between the two parts of Great Britain. Pitt's Free Trade policy was distinctly unpopular. His attempt to relieve the Catholics from political disabilities drove him from office. There is every reason to suppose that the followers of Lord George Gordon represented the predominant religious sentiment both of England & of Scotland. The governing classes were more tolerant & enlightened than the people.

But the Constitution, though not democratic, was national. The paradox, though it remains rather a paradox than an established fact, that the unreformed Parliament represented the various classes in the nation more truly than could any representative assembly formed on a purely democratic model, contains an element of truth. The nomination boroughs did in fact open a career to men of talent to whom since the abolition of close boroughs public life has been more or less closed, and a limited number of constituencies, such, for example as Westminster, which contained more than 20,000 electors provided a means which hardly existed under the Reform Act of 1832 for giving expression to the sentiment or the prejudices of the mass of the people. The Constitution, in short, did on the whole enable the classes who took an interest in politics, and these may from a political point of view be fairly termed the nation, to make known, & in the long run enforce their will. It was the gradual shifting of population wealth & power towards the North of England which, combined with other circumstances, made the old Constitution cease to represent the nation & which thus caused the passing of the great Reform Act.

4. *The Executive, by which for the present purpose must be understood the Cabinet when fully supported by the Crown, possessed a kind of independence unknown to modern Ministers.*

It was possible for the Government to defy prevalent opinion. The contest with Wilkes,[102] the suppression of Gordon Riots, & of the movement of which it formed part, the execution of Dr Dodd, the peace of 1761, we may even say the concession of legislative independence to Ireland in 1782, all bear witness in different ways to the freedom with which the Executive could act. In some of these cases the Government was, in the opinion of most modern critics, in the wrong, whilst in others it was in the right, but my immediate point is not that the Executive was wiser or more foolish than the people, but that the Executive was more or less independent. It has been already pointed out that the Crown & the Ministry which generally, it must be remarked, was connected with, & commanded therefore the influence of certain noble families, had means for guiding & controlling the action of the House of Commons. They were not nearly so liable as have been some Cabinets of later times, to be thrown out of office by loss of popularity in the House.

5. *Parliament itself possessed a large amount of independence.*

The true Whig theory, as represented by Burke is that Parliament was no merely representative assembly, but was the sovereign. This is of course the theory of English law. It is, as has been often pointed out, the only logical vindication for the passing of the Septennial Act.[103] But in the 18th century the theory of parliamentary sovereignty corresponded much more nearly than it does at present with political facts. Within certain limits hard to be defined, but which were very real Parliament, that is the King, Lords, & Commons, did really & habitually exercise supreme power. Frequent

102 [John Wilkes (1725–97), popular London politician and radical journalist. –Ed.]

103 [The Septennial Act, passed in December 1716, prolonged the life of the 1715 Parliament from three years to seven. – Ed.]

or unexpected dissolutions were all but unknown & though a dissolution might no doubt change the balance of parties, it did not, as it does now, make the seat of every M.P. unsafe. Dissolution or no dissolution the patrons of the nomination boroughs retained their power, & their nominees retained their seats whatever were the changes in public opinion.

6. Limit to the sphere of the State's activity.

We should always remember that men are after all ruled by their opinions or beliefs, though their opinions are generally determined by their interests or their supposed interests. Now both the working & the spirit of the Constitution was in periods with which we are dealing essentially influenced by an opinion, we might almost say habit, which for good & bad has more or less passed away or at any rate temporarily has ceased to exert its former power. This opinion was in effect that the State was called upon to protect men's personal safety, freedom, & property, but ought to act within a very limited sphere. No doubt the theory of *laissey faire* was in the time of George the Third not formulated either by statesmen or by the public & there were large portions of English social life which represented so to speak, survivals of other opinions. The Established Church, the Poor Law, the legislative protection of different interests all depended for their existence or justification on the opinion that the State ought to intervene in many things beyond the protection of person & property. But the habit of the governing classes was to leave things alone. There was little legislative reform or legislative innovation. To put the matter at the very lowest, the legislative & administrative powers of the State were not used to effect changes. Whole departments of government, such for example as the Education Office, as the Local Government Board, as the Police, are of modern creation. They all bear witness to a revolution of ideas. Inactivity was the characteristic of the English government under George III. This inactivity favoured the growth of abuses, it favoured also the development of individual freedom.

6

Memorandum on Party Government
(July 1898)

Introduction

Every one is influenced by inconsistent feelings with regard to government by Party.

On the one hand we are prone, in England at least, to assume that Party government is an essential characteristic of popular, or at any rate of Parliamentary government, and publicists often attribute the real or alleged failure of parliamentary government in France, or in Italy to the absence of defined parties, the lack whereof makes it impossible to establish true Party government as it exists in England.[104]

It is even asserted that the Party system is probably the strongest purifying agent in Parliamentary government under extended suffrage.[105] This assertion indeed sounds an extravagant paradox to anyone who reflects on the condition of affairs at New York. Yet we all perceive that in someway or other there is a close connexion between the Party system & Parliamentary government as it has existed in England for about two centuries, & further that certain definite evils arise when parties break up into groups each representing different interests or different ideas.

104 See Bodley, *France*, pp. 76, 163–165, 297 [J.E.C. Bodley, *France* (London, 1898). – Ed.] Lowell, *Governments & Parties*, pp. 69, 70, 72 [A. Lowell, *Governments and Parties in Continental Europe* (Cambridge, Mass.), 1896. – Ed.]

105 Bodley, p. 297.

On the other hand, no one can help feeling that there is a sense in which government by Party is an evil, even though it be necessary evil. Most persons are at times haunted by the desire for a condition of feeling under which "none are for a faction and all are for the state". There is something irrational in the supposition that for the promotion of good government it is essentially necessary that there should be a constant conflict between the men in office & the men out of office or that, as Maine[106] has somewhere put it, the sixteen ablest men in Parliament should be employed to carry on the administration of the country's affairs, and the sixteen next ablest men in Parliament should be employed in hindering them in the administration of the country's affairs. Nor is it possible for any student to disguise from himself that the party system is a comparatively new phenomenon, & that countries have been & are well governed in which that system does not in reality exist; consider for instance Cobden's[107] eulogy [*sic*] of Prussian administration in 1835, and the prosperity of modern Switzerland where party government of the English type has not been developed.

The problem before us is how to reconcile this apparent contradiction in men's feelings as to government by Party.

My purpose is to see if this reconciliation can be achieved by examining, first, what is meant by the Party system, secondly, what, if you take that system at its best, are its merits and defects, thirdly, what are the conditions under which it can work for good; fourthly, what are the evils which the absence of these conditions produces, and fifthly, to what extent the Party system can be dispensed with under a Parliamentary constitution.

106 [Sir Henry James Sumner Maine (1822–88), jurist, appointed Regius Professor of Civil Law at Cambridge (1847). His *Popular Government* (Cambridge, 1885) attracted much criticism. – Ed.]

107 [Richard Cobden (1804–65), liberal politician. – Ed.]

A. Meaning of the Party system.

Those who write about the Party system have in view the form of Party government which has existed, or is assumed to have existed in England at any rate for the last hundred years.

In England during this period there have existed two main parties whom for the sake of convenience one may call Tories & Whigs or Conservatives & Liberals, who have been, or have supposed themselves to be influenced by different principles of government & have been represented in Parliament by the Government or the Opposition as the case might be. Each of these have constituted distinct parliamentary parties under the leadership of known parliamentary leaders: whose object it was to enforce as far as possible their own policy & to oppose the policy of their opponents. The leaders moreover of each party have been prepared to conduct the government of the country when called upon to do so by the Crown which was itself guided in its choice of servants more or less directly by the wishes of the House of Commons. The Tories for example when in power conducted the administration of public affairs, including in that term all important parliamentary legislation, in accordance with Tory principles. The Whigs if in opposition made it their main effort to turn the Tories out of power and if they failed in this to introduce into the conduct of affairs as much of Whig principles as they could enforce upon their political opponents. The result of course has been that on a change of government there ensued or was supposed to ensue a change of principle. The place of each party was reversed; the Tories, e.g. (in 1830) passing from the party of the government into the place of the Opposition, & the Whigs becoming the Ministry of the day or, in other words, the Government.

B. Apparent Advantages of System.

The different ways in which the system above described, facilitates the action of parliamentary government have often been dwelt upon & are pretty obvious.

The existence throughout the country & in Parliament of two organised bodies each linked together by common principles & each prepared to support their leaders when in office is a guarantee against the kind of anarchy into which parties, whether in or out of Parliament break up when they are not held together by strict discipline. The influence of the party exerted through its leaders, may no doubt often or at any rate sometimes be a check upon the selfishness or treachery of individuals. In estimating the merits & demerits of connections based on partisanship it must be remembered that men may fall below as they may rise above, loyalty to their associates.

If you examine for example the career of the class of adventurer of whom Wedderburn[108] was, in the last century, a fair type you see clearly enough that it required all the power of party discipline in which one must include the natural sympathies inspired by comradeship to prevent unscrupulous politicians from turning public life into a mere game for the promotion of their own interests. Burke's arguments in favour of Party at bottom amount to this; that is in the earlier years of George III nothing but honourable adherence to Party connections would enable average politicians to act in accordance with principle. The charge against George, & in a measure against Pitt, was that their attempt to break up Party resulted in leading politicians to forsake their principles for their interests.

The Party system, in the next place, put the administration in the hands of well known leaders, who whatever their defects, must have been able to

108 [Sir William Wedderburn (1838–1918), administrator and political reformer, dedicated supporter of India's political aspirations.– Ed.]

produce an impression upon Parliament, & especially upon the House of Commons. At lowest they were men possessed of talents which rendered them distinguished in an assembly which contained many of the wisest the most capable & the most influential men in England. They were persons qualified to be leaders of men. Under the Party system bad men might be in power. It was hardly possible that office should long be held by nonentities. If you take the English Cabinets which have held office since George the Third came to the throne you will find that they contained members of considerably more than average ability.

The existence further of two parties each of whose leaders were prepared to take office had two good results. There were never lacking a body of persons by whom the Government might be carried on; and the Government was checked & prevented from committing errors by the criticism of the Opposition & the censures of the Opposition were moderated by the knowledge that the censors might at any moment be called upon to undertake the responsibility of carrying on the Government.[109]

If, lastly, you may assume that, as no doubt was often the case, Tories & Whigs really advocated essentially different principles it then follows that the Party system is, or may be based upon fundamental differences of conviction & that the maintenance of Party connections was in reality a means of keeping the conduct of average men in harmony with their conscientious beliefs.

109 The security against bad government afforded by the criticism of an Opposition may be greatly exaggerated. Just because an Opposition must be ex officio censors deprives their criticism of weight. A more serious defect not sufficiently noted is that the feelings or interests of the Government & the Opposition may often coincide, & that, when this is so, the supposed security against bad government ceases. The High Churchmanship of Lord Salisbury & of Mr Gladstone has, combined with other causes, given undue weight for the last 30 years to the High Church party. An opposition again which may itself come into office is almost as unwilling as the Government to do anything which may check the freedom of a ministry as to appointments & therefore does very little in the way of criticising jobbery.

So much at any rate may be granted to the advocates of the Party system that in more ways than one it facilitates the regular & beneficial action of Parliamentary government.

Note however that even in England theory of Party system never perfectly carried out in fact. Considerable disagreements of principle exist among members of same party, e.g. as to "Catholic" question, 1820–1829, measures carried by party which has opposed them, e.g. Catholic Relief, 1829; Repeal of Corn Laws, 1845.

C. Inherent Demerits of Party System.

These are clearly seen, if we take system in England at about its best 1832–1845.

1. It makes impossible consideration of measures on merits.

Peel was the best administrator of his age, & no one can doubt that many of subordinate Whig reforms which he or his followers delayed, e. g. institution of County Courts would have been promoted by himself if in office.

2. An Opposition which cannot carry out its own policy maims & renders abortive the policy of the Government.

This [is] illustrated by the political history of 1832–1841. Most persons would now grant that the Irish policy of the Whigs was on the whole sound. Every one would concede that if it were to be tried it ought to have been tried fairly. Yet the history of the opposition as to the Irish Church, as to Irish municipal government, as to collection of tithes in Ireland, as to the relation between the government, & O'Connell,[110] is nothing but an account of successful attempts to delay & embarrass a policy which the opposition could not reverse. To sum the matter up shortly Peel was the ablest Parliamentary leader of his time. His administrative capacity & the circumstance that he twice carried through popular reforms, have given him the reputation of a reformer, yet, under the influence of the Party system, his substantial work as a leader was to delay reforms till they became all but useless.

3. *The Party system involves a waste of capacity.*

Peel & his immediate followers were the best administrators in England. The public lost the use of their administrative powers because the Whigs, who were poor administrators, pursued on the whole the policy approved by the nation, whilst Peel advocated, or was supposed to advocate, a policy opposed to that of the Whigs.

4. *The Party system leads to an exaggeration of the points on which the whole of one party, e.g. the Tories, are supposed to agree & to be opposed to the whole of their opponents, e.g. the Whigs.*

It is to say the least very dubious whether between 1832 & 1845 the differences which divided the Conservative leaders from the Whig leaders, were most of them very serious could they irrespective of the Party system have been formed into a Board or Cabinet for carrying on the business of the nation, such as is the Swiss Council, it is quite conceivable that Peel,

110 [Daniel O'Connell (1775–1847), first of the great nineteenth-century Irish leaders in the House of Commons. – Ed.]

Lyndhurst,[111] & the Duke of Wellington[112] might have acted harmoniously together with Melbourne,[113] Lord John Russell[114] & Macaulay.[115]

Hence further, not only political leaders but the whole of a party, come to think that the party to which they belong is made up of good men & that the party to which they are opposed is made up of bad men, whence partisans come to hold that their own party, especially if it has been long in office, has a moral right to be in power, & that there is something shocking to the national conscience in a transfer of authority from a party which has long held sway to their opponents. This was the feeling of the Whigs in 1760; it was the feeling of the Tories in 1829, it became the feeling of the Liberals in 1886. What makes this state of sentiment the more dangerous is that it is often based on a certain amount of fact. It will be found, if you look at English history, that from time to time the morality of the nation has in truth been in the main represented by a given political party. Thus in 1783 & for at least thirty or forty years longer, the men who most deserved national confidence & respect did in fact belong to the Tories, & though it is more difficult to speak with certainty of later times it is maintainable that on the whole, from, say 1845–1865 the moral force of the country belonged to the Liberals, including in that term Whigs, Peelites & Radicals. But though this shifting of moral respectability from one party to another is a noticeable fact, it still is true that the party system intensifies the tendency of politicians & their followers to look upon their own side as the party of the good, & upon the opposite side as a faction of bad men,

111 [John Singleton Copley, Baron Lyndhurst (1772–1863), politician, lord chancellor, 1827–30. – Ed.]

112 [Arthur Wellesley, 1st Duke of Wellington (1769–1852), prime minister, 1828–30. – Ed.]

113 [William Lamb, 2nd Viscount Melbourne (1779–1848), prime minister, 1834, 1835–41. – Ed.]

114 [Lord John Russell (1792–1878), prime minister, 1846–52, 1865–6. – Ed.]

115 [Lord Thomas Babington Macaulay (1800–59), historian, MP, spoke in support of the reform of Parliament (Reform Bill of 1831), Secretary at War in Melbourne's Cabinet (1839). – Ed.]

whence, among other evils, results the sort of political hypocrisy which leads men of sense & merit to overlook or palliate the decline in moral principle of a party which they have at one time held, perhaps rightly, to represent public virtue.

The patent evils, in short, of the Party system even at its best, are that it presents men from considering measures on their own merits, that it produces that kind of vicious compromise by which an opposition maims a policy which it cannot resist, that it involves a waste of political capacity, that it exaggerates the differences which divide one party from another & promotes the idea which is often false, & at best only partially true, that one party in the State has a monopoly of public virtue.

These, be it noted, are not so much the corruptions of government by party, as understood in England, but rather its inherent faults, & these faults have, even where the party system under the guidance of men such as Sir Robert Peel, Lord Althorp,[116] or Lord John Russell, assumed its best form, worked great evil to England. Let us for a moment however lay aside the defects of the party system and assuming that on the whole they are over-balanced by its merits, examine:

116 [John Charles Spencer, Lord Althorp (1782–1845), leader of the House of Commons & chancellor of the exchequer, 1830–4. – Ed.]

D. The Conditions Necessary for the Beneficial Action of the Party System.

These conditions are, speaking broadly, four:

1st Condition: *All parties in the State must be loyal to the Constitution.*

Government by Party, in the English sense of the terms, can hardly exist, or at any rate cannot produce its best results if any considerable body of citizens are disloyal to the Constitution, & are prepared to overthrow it by force or intrigue, or even are so completely hostile to it that they will take no part in the administering the government of the country, & do not wish to promote the proper working of its institutions.

This state of things is an absolutely essential condition for the proper working of the Party system and this for an obvious reason. If in a given country a large number of persons are revolutionists or reactionists prepared if necessary to change the Constitution, it is impossible that they or their leaders should be admitted to power, for the moment they came into office they would use the authority of the state not for carrying on the administration of affairs but for carrying out a revolution. To take an extreme case it was absolutely impossible under the Commonwealth or the Protectorate to put the Government in the hands of Cavaliers or even of moderate Presbyterians since it was certain that they would use power to effect a restoration, and in passing one may note that the real reason why the Puritan Revolution failed is that the revolutionary government even when in the hands of Cromwell, did not command the loyal adherence of large portions of the nation so again up till 1760 it was practically impossible to bring the Tory party, though probably it represented the majority of the nation, into office, and the Septennial Act was in truth a pacific *coup d'etat* by which the Whigs guarded against the chance of that what we should now call the swing of the pendulum, or in other words the regular operation of the Party system should give a parliamentary majority to

Tories who would destroy the revolution settlement. Exactly the same difficulty beset the government who after the first violence of the first French Revolution was passed, tried to establish something like orderly freedom. They had introduced the Party system & yet could not trust its operation since it might at any moment place in office reactionists who would overthrow the Constitution. The *coup d'etat* of 13 Vendémiaire (5 Aug. 1795) as also of 18 Fructedor (4 Sept. 1797) were both caused or justified by the necessity for arresting the triumph of the party which might lead to the overthrow of the Republic.

It were easy to give other examples of the obvious fact that disloyalty to the constitution on the part of a large party in a given country makes the regular operation of the Party system impossible. It is worth note however that the proper action of party is inconsistent not only with active disloyalty or conspiracy, but also with the negative disloyalty which takes the form of abstention from political life. Republican government in France suffers from the attitude of the Legitimists or reactionists; the constitutional monarchy of Italy rests on an unsound foundation because all genuine Catholics, that is all Italians who in political matters are guided by the Pope, abstain from taking part in parliamentary elections. The reason again why the system of obstruction organised by Mr Parnell[117] intensely alarmed English statesmen is that it made patent the existence of a disciplined party which was morally disloyal to the constitution. Even if we put aside every question as to the connection between the Parnellite opposition & Fenians or dynamiters, this at any rate must be admitted. The aim of Parnellite obstruction was to frustrate the conduct of business in Parliament. It was disloyalty using for its ends not arms but parliamentary forms. Like other forms of rebellion it may have had its justification. On that point I say nothing, all I maintain is that it struck at the root of the Party system.

117 [Charles Stewart Parnell (1846–91), leader of the struggle for Irish Home Rule, Irish nationalist member of the House of Commons, 1875–91. –Ed.]

It will be granted that substantial loyalty to the Constitution on the part at any rate of that portion of the citizens who take a real part in public life, is an essential condition for the proper working of the Party system. What Englishmen, & I think Americans fail to note is the rarity with which this condition is fulfilled. It is only during a very short portion of the modern history of England that it has existed in Great Britain. It does not exist at present moment in France, in Italy or Spain. It does not exist in the Austrian Empire. Whether it exists in the German Empire may be doubtful. There are only two continental countries where we can confidentially say that loyalty to the constitution flourishes. These countries are Belgium & Switzerland. The Belgian system we may add is about the most satisfactory reproduction of the English Constitution & of the English Party system to be found in Europe. Switzerland is the most successful of European democracies but in Switzerland, though we find one of the conditions requisite for the Party system thoroughly fulfilled government by party is unknown.

2nd Condition: *The distinction between the two parties in the State must depend upon real differences of principle.*

There exists on the face of things a great difficulty in ensuring the combined existence of our first & our second condition. In other words, the Party system implies that a nation should not be divided by differences of political creed which can be described on the one side as loyalty & on the other side as disloyalty to the constitution but that the nation is divided by differences of principle sufficiently marked to form the basis of real parties. What is needed, in short, is a very singular state of opinion which may be described as one of agreement as to fundamentals combined with disagreement as to matters of essential importance which are not fundamentals. If one may borrow ecclesiastical forms and apply them to political life, one may say that the Party system requires at once the absence of schism & the presence both of orthodoxy & of heterodoxy.

Let however this primary difficulty of combining fundamental agreement with really important disagreement be dismissed from consideration. Yet when this is done it will still be found that the necessity for basing Party organisation on true differences of opinion of itself makes the maintenance of Party government a matter by no means easy to achieve.

Differences of principle which at one time were real, may from the course of events or the turn of opinion come to an end. Up till 1745 England was more or less divided into Whigs who supported & Tories who disapproved of the revolution settlement. The rebellion of that year terminated all real change [*sic*] of a Jacobite restoration. On the accession of George III fifteen years later, men found to their surprise that Jacobitism was dead, & that the substantial difference which had divided them was at an end. For more than a century the political world of Europe has been divided under different names & in different forms into promoters & the opponents of Democracy. We are just beginning to perceive that the spread of democratic principles is rendering this basis of division unmeaning. This does not mean that men are agreed on the solution of all or even of the most important of political problems. What it does mean is that the old lines of divisions are out of date. In Switzerland, for example, & the United States, & with some qualifications one might add in England the distinction between Democrats & Anti-democrats has little real import. The old foundations of Party division are obsolete & for the moment the existence therefore of Parties based on principles is almost an impossibility.

The same result follows from a different cause.

Where a large number of citizens are disloyal to the constitution & either conspire against it or refuse to take any part in public life the "loyalists" who of course in a Republic would be Republicans as under a constitutional Monarchy they would be constitutionalists, are compelled to act together & to exclude the "disloyalists" (if one may use such a term) from office. This it may be noted is at the present moment the state of things in France & in Italy, just as it was the political condition of Great Britain between the accession of the Hanoverian dynasty, 1714, to the accession of George III, 1760. Hence followed two consequences. There is no real Party system, the men in power inevitably belong to one only of the two great political divisions in the country, e.g. in the case of modern France to the Republicans. But in the next place there is certain to spring up a sort of false Party system, i.e. more struggles for office between the different divisions or groups of predominant party. This is one explanation of the constant changes of French cabinets. One unknown ministry succeeds another equally unknown, just because there is no real difference between the Opposition & the Government. They are of necessity factions of the Republican party. Exactly the same phenomenon, though it showed itself in a different form, was seen in England during a great part of the 18th century.

3rd Condition: *Parties must not be kept together mainly by personal interest.*

The legitimate Party system depends upon the existence of real divisions of political opinion. From the moment that the main tie which binds Parties together is personal interest, under which term one ought perhaps to include mere personal partisanship, the true foundation of Party government is undermined. Yet when for any reason whatever the other requirements of the Party system do not exist, it is almost certain that the attempt will be made to keep parties together by motives of self interest which in the last resort amount to corruption. The downright bribery of Walpole, the lavish expenditure which kept together the King's Friends, the "austere corruption" of Guizot[118] all at bottom arose from the same cause. They were all attempts to keep together parties by appeals to private interest.[119]

118 [François Guizot (1787–1874), French politician and historian, prominent minister in France during the July Monarchy, 1830–48. – Ed.]

119 Walpole's bribery was the most respectable, as it was the most successful form of corruption. It could more or less be defended by, as it owed its success to the consideration that Walpole & the best of his supporters though they secured power by dubious means yet were a real party bound together by common principles & pursu-

4th Condition: *There must if possible exist only two important parties.*

It is not indeed necessary for the fulfilment of this condition that these parties should not themselves be divided into smaller groups, but it is necessary that they should be groups strictly within each of the parties & that the difference dividing any group from the rest of the party to which it belongs should be felt by the members of such group to be less important than the difference dividing the two parties.

The Party system as a means of Parliamentary government cannot work to any good effect if Parliament itself is divided into small groups or bodies each of which works for its own end with little regard to the ends aimed at by the whole party to which it professedly belongs. This is so obvious & is nowadays so constantly noted that the point is hardly worth working out. But it is well to observe that breaking of parties into groups may arise from one of two different causes.

It may be due to fanaticism, that is excessive & disproportionate zeal for the attainment of some special end, e.g. Free Trade, Temperance, Anti-vaccination, & the like. If a body of politicians are willing to support any party whatever which will favour the particular cause, be it good or bad, which such politicians wish to succeed, then, as far as they are concerned, the Party system is at an end. If twenty members of Parliament are induced by the promise of a Protective tariff, of Free Trade, or of a Local Option Act, to support a given party, whatever be its other principle then the Party system is, as far as these twenty members are concerned, at an end. Their motives may be excellent, but their action enables one of two parties which *ex hypothesi* does not fairly command a majority to gain office.[120]

---

ing a legitimate end, viz. the maintenance of the Hanoverian succession on which ultimately depended the maintenance of English liberty.

120 This statement must be taken subject to one limitation; a particular measure, e.g. the Reform Bill of 1832, may involve so many general questions of policy as to form the basis of a new division into two parties. In this case the supporters of such a measure may readjust instead of destroying, the Party system.

The breaking up into groups may, on the other hand, be due to self interest. If, to take an extreme case twenty members of Parliament were willing to sell their votes to either of the great parties for place or pay, these members would as far as lay in them, break up the Party system.

Look at the matter which way you will the rise of separate groups or factions pursuing their own ends without regard to the principles of the party to which they ally themselves is fatal to any beneficial system of Party government.

5th Condition: *The nation must take a real interest in politics.*

This perhaps ought to have been put forward as the primary & most essential condition for the proper working of Party government. Popular government, & certainly parliamentary government, will never work well – it will scarcely work at all in a country where men are not really interested in politics. If the electors have no real care as to the political conduct of their representatives it is absolutely certain that Parliament will be governed by factions kept together by self interest & intrigue. The statement that the nation must be interested in politics requires however some explanation. For our present purpose it is not necessary that the whole of a nation should be politicians. The Party government existed & in some respects worked well in England between 1714 & 1832, yet whilst Parliament was unreformed large classes had nothing to do with the government of the country & presumably took little interest in it. The same thing was more or less true of large bodies of the people between 1832 & 1884. But what is really meant by the assertion that the nation must be interested in politics is that the portion of a state which holds political power, the "legal country", to adopt a French expression, should be interested. The best feature in English public life has been the constant interest of the electors in political question. Faction though more reviled, is far less dangerous than indifference.[121]

121 Contrast the small interest taken in politics by the French electorate. A practical moral suggested by our 5th condition is the peril of extending political rights to classes devoid of political interest.

E. Evils from Failure of Conditions.

The Party system has at its best defects which have been already noted but in addition to these there flow from party government several distinct evils which may be fairly attributed to the failure of the conditions on which the good working of the Party system depends.

These evils may take different forms. They may be the obvious sacrifice of public interest to party spirit – the tendency to create questions or, to use the popular expression, cries, which may cause the kind of division in opinion needed for the existence of parties [*sic*],[122] or actual corruption or bribery. But all these evils may be summed up under one head whenever they exist they mean that parties are degenerating into factions, that is to say that they have become, or are becoming, bodies of men not bound together by community of principles but either by self interest or by the feeling of partisanship.

F. How far can the Party system be dispensed with & what are its mitigations?

It is perfectly plain that the Party system as it has existed for the last 150 years or so in England, is not a necessary part of parliamentary government. In England it has been in existence (historically speaking) for only a short time, that is for not more than a century & a half, & even during this period it has not been fully developed. Till 1832 the crowd exerted

122 No sensible man can doubt that again & again political controversies have been raised in England mainly for the sake of keeping a party together. One reason why Parliamentary reform excited legitimate alarm in the minds of many men who were not strong Tories, was the perception that changes in the Constitution would henceforth be advocated for the sake of keeping a party together.

great influence independently of Party. At times moreover, e.g. from 1800 to 1820, the opposition was generally so feeble in numbers & weight that the Party system as now understood, existed rather in name than in reality, & in comparatively recent times, e.g. between 1860 & 1865, the party in office has been in fact supported by a large number of nominal opponents so that the Government possessed in reality rather a national than a party support. Switzerland, again, which is the most successful of modern Democracies, possesses parliamentary government without the support of the Party system.

Party government in short though in many countries on all but inseparable accident is not an essential property of parliamentary government. Still in England at least the Party system is so well established that its continuance must be taken for granted, & the part of wisdom is not to place its abolition but to consider what are, or may be its mitigations.

These are some of the most obvious.

1. The judicial[123] & administrative bodies of the country should be kept as far as possible beyond the sphere of Party.

123 The appointment of Judges from among the leading members of a particular party is an evil mainly because it militates against the promotion to the Bench of the best lawyers on account of legal merit, though the appointment of law officers to judicial places is an advantage since it results in the Bench being filled by the real leaders of the Bar, but though the appointment of e.g. conservatives as judges by Conservative Chancellor is a slight evil, since a judge appointed by Tories need not become a Tory judge. Nothing can be imagined more noxious than the appointment of judges as partisans, i.e, as representatives of a Party on the Bench. The idea has been broached & acted upon that the magistrates of a county ought to represent in certain proportions the political parties which exist there. The idea, if true, applies logically to every Court in the Kingdom. It is however totally false, & those who wish the deterioration of the Party system should oppose every suggestion for the representation of parties on the Bench. One of the leading errors of the day is the misapplication of the doctrine of representation; in the discharge of official duties the primary thing to look to is not representative character but capacity & as regards judicial functions, capacity includes an independence of Party which is inconsistent with the representation of a Party.

This has in fact been to a great extent achieved both in England & in Belgium where alone the Party system has worked satisfactorily. In both countries partisans may be made judges but the judges are not partisans.

In both countries the Civil Service has taken no part in politics, & at the present day appointments to the Civil Service are in England at least little, if at all, dependent upon political favour. Civil Servants moreover though for the most part legally dismissible, in practice hold their offices by a tenure nearly as certain as that of the judges. The independence of the Civil Service has been one main though unnoticed cause of the success of Party government in England.[124]

It were further well to consider whether some of the cabinet offices might not be held by men who were independent of Party. The questions which come before a Lord Chancellor either as a judge or as a minister of Justice, have generally but slight connection with party differences & the nation would gain could lawyer who discharged well the duties of the Chancellor hold office in Cabinets of different political colours. The same thing may perhaps be said about the Minister for Foreign Affairs. But here we touch upon a different point.

2. Large questions of general policy should whenever possible be so determined that they may be placed outside the realm of party.

Some examples will show my meaning. When Peel accepted the results of the Reform Bill, he placed the changes introduced by the measure of 1832 beyond discussion. Between 1800 & 1886 the Union with Ireland was supported by each party in the State. As far as Great Britain was concerned Repeal was not a Party question. So again for the last 50 years Free Trade

124 Note that where the long predominance of one party in power has filled the leading places in the Civil Service which men in the main belonging to one party there have occasionally been signs that the Party system has not worked well. One may suspect that the administrative failures of Whigs between 1832 & 1845 were in part due to want of zealous support by Tory officials. Nor is it certain that in 1852, or perhaps later Disraeli & his colleagues did not suffer some inconveniences from the political bias of the permanent civil servants.

has been the settled policy of England. It has been placed outside the realm of Party. A main object of patriotic statesmanship should be to increase the number of matters which could not become the subject of party difference. On all the main points of national concern there ought in short to be a traditional policy to which each party in the State should adhere. It is certainly not past hope that the time may arrive when the number of closed questions may be so great that the Party system may work & work well, within a limited area.

G. What then is the explanation of the contradiction which is to be found in most people's feelings with regard to the Party system?

The answer is this: The conditions necessary for the beneficial working of the Party system are also the requirements under which alone popular government can flourish. Thus loyalty to the Constitution, an active interest in public affairs among the mass of the citizens, the management of national business by leading men of marked talent & of high character, & the like, are all conditions required for the satisfactory working of the Party system, & they are also the necessary requirements of popular governments. The Party system therefore when at its best is a sign, though it is not a cause, of the good health of the State. And Englishmen at any rate attribute to Party itself benefits which really flow from partisanship but from the circumstances which make political partisanship innocuous. Hence the idea that the Party system is itself beneficial.

The moment however that the conditions of healthy party contests or, in other words, the conditions required for the healthiness of popular government cease to exist, it becomes obvious to every one that Party, which is then called the spirit of faction, is the destruction, not the salvation of the Commonwealth. Men then begin to deprecate party spirit & condemn the Party system.

If this be the true answer to the question before us it leads to an important result. Patriotic statesmanship need take no trouble to maintain the Party system where it is established, & still less to create it where it is unknown. Their whole effort should be devoted to maintaining or nurturing the requirements of good popular government. It may happen that under certain circumstances the maintenance of these requirements may for a time give rise to party government.

It is equally possible that under other circumstances the maintenance of these requirements may destroy the Party system. The diffusion for example of loyalty to Republican institutions throughout the whole French people might it is possible in France give birth to bona fide Party government, but it might also inaugurate a system like that of Switzerland, or even resembling that of Prussia which ensured freedom & popular government without invoking the aid of parties. It is always to be borne in mind that Burke, who was the most systematic defender of the Party system himself towards the end of his life, destroyed the Party organisations of his day. As in most of Burke's conduct we have here an apparent inconsistency arising from passionate adherence to one consistent principle. Burke's eulogy of Party meant that in his judgement the morality of public life could in 1766 be maintained only by the loyal adherence of honest men to their Party principles. His appeal to the old Whigs & their consequent union with the Tories, meant that in 1794 the break up of the Party system was necessary for the maintenance of public morality & loyalty to the Constitution. In 1766 & in 1794 Burke, assuming that his view of the facts was correct, defended the conditions of sound popular government. [Page missing.]

Select Bibliography

Abbott, W.C. (ed.), *The Writings and Speeches of Oliver Cromwell*, 4 vols, Cambridge, Mass., 1937–47.

Adams, G.B., *The Origin of the English Constitution*, New Haven, CT, 1912.

Allan, T., *Law, Liberty and Justice*, Oxford, 1993.

Austin, J., *The Province of Jurisprudence Determined*, ed. H.L.A. Hart, London, 1954.

Bagehot, W., *The English Constitution*, London, 1878.

Baker, J.H., *An Introduction to English Legal History*, 3rd edn, London, 1990.

Barlow, F., *The Feudal Kingdom of England 1042–1216*, 5th edn, London, 1999.

Barnett, H., *Constitutional and Administrative Law*, 3rd edn, London, 2000.

Bicknell, B.A., *Cases on Constitutional Law*, Oxford, 1925.

Blackstone, W., *Commentaries on the Laws of England*, 4 vols, Oxford, 1765.

Bodley, J.E.C., *France*, London, 1898.

Bogdanor, V., *The Monarchy and the Constitution*, Oxford, 1995.

Boutmy, E., *Etudes de Droit Constitionnel: France–Angleterre–Etats Unis*, Paris, 1885.

Bradley, A.W., and Ewing, K.D., *Constitutional and Administrative Law*, 12th edn, London, 1997.

Bryce, J., *The American Commonwealth*, London, 1893.

Burke, E., *The Writings and Speeches of Edmund Burke*, ed. P. Langford, Oxford, 1981–2000.

Burrows, N., *Devolution*, London, 2000.

Campbell, G. (8th Duke of Argyll), *The New British Constitution and Its Master Builders*, Edinburgh, 1888.

Collini, S., *The Public Moralists*, Oxford, 1993.

Collini, S., Winch, D., and Burrow, J., *That Noble Science of Politics: A Study in Nineteenth-Century Intellectual History*, Cambridge, 1983.

Costin, W.C., and Steven Watson, J., *The Law and Working of the Constitution. Documents 1660–1914*, London, 1953.

Craig, P.P., *Administrative Law*, 5th edn, London, 2003.

Denning, Lord, *Landmarks in the Law*, London, 1984.

Dicey, A.V., *A Treatise on the Rules for the Selection of the Parties to an Action*, London, 1870.

Dicey, A.V., *Introduction to the Study of the Law of the Constitution*, London, 1885.

Dicey, A.V., *Lectures on the Relation between Law and Public Opinion in England during the Nineteenth Century*, London, 1905.

Gardiner, S., *History of England 1603–42*, London, 1883–4.

Gardiner, S., *Constitutional Documents of the Puritan Revolution*, London, 1899.

Gash, N., *Aristocracy and People, England 1815–1865*, London, 1979.

Goldsworthy, J., *The Sovereignty of Parliament: History and Philosophy*, Oxford, 1999.

Green, T.H., *Collected Works*, ed. L. Nettleship, London, 1885–8.

Greenleaf, W.H., *The British Political Tradition*: *The Rise of Collectivism*, London, 1983.

Hallam, H., *The Constitutional History of England from the Accession of Henry VII to the Death of George II*, 2 vols, London, 1827.

Hearn, W., *The Government of England, its Structure and its Development*, London, 1867.

Hobbes, T., *Leviathan*, ed. M.J. Oakeshott, Oxford, 1955.

Holdsworth, W., *A History of English Law*, eds A.L. Goodhart and H.G. Hanbury, London, 1964.

Hood Phillips, O., *Constitutional and Administrative Law*, 7th edn, London, 1987.

Jennings, Sir I., *The Law and the Constitution*, London, 1933.

Jennings, Sir I., *Cabinet Government*, 2nd edn, Cambridge, 1951.

Johnson, N., *In Search of the Constitution*, London, 1977.

Jolliffe, J.E.A., *The Constitutional History of Medieval England*, London, 1952.

Jowell, J., and Oliver, D., *The Changing Constitution*, Oxford, 2007.
Keir, Sir D.L., *The Constitutional History of Modern Britain 1485–1951*, 5th edn, London, 1953.
Kenyon, J.P., *The Stuart Constitution*, Cambridge, 1986.
Kim, K., *Aliens in Medieval Law: The Origins of Modern Citizenship*, Cambridge, 2000.
King, A., *The British Constitution*, London, 2008.
Laski, H., *The Grammar of Politics*, London, 1925.
Leyland, P., *The Constitution of the United Kingdom*, Oxford, 2007.
Lockwood, S. (ed.), *On the Laws and Governance of England*, Cambridge, 1997.
Loughlin, M., *Public Law and Political Theory*, Oxford, 2003.
Loveland, I., *Constitutional Law: A Critical Introduction*, London, 1996.
Lowell, A., *Governments and Parties in Continental Europe*, Cambridge, Mass., 1896.
Lyon, A., *Constitutional History of the United Kingdom*, London, 2003.
Macaulay, T.B., *Critical Historical Essays*, London, 1850.
Mackintosh, J.P., *The British Cabinet*, London, 1962.
Maine, H.J., *Popular Government*, Cambridge, 1885.
Maitland, F.W., *The Constitutional History of England*, Cambridge, 1911.
McKechnie, W.S., *Magna Carta*, Glasgow, 1905.
Montesquieu, C. de, *De l'Esprit des Lois*, Paris, 1750.
Musson, A., and Ormrod, W.M., *The Evolution of English Justice: Law, Politics and Society in the Fourteenth Century*, London, 1999.
Nolan, Lord, and Sedley, Sir S. (eds), *The Making and Remaking of the British Constitution*, London, 1997.
Oldfield, T., *History of the Original Constitution of Parliaments*, London, 1797.
Paley, W., *The Principles of Moral and Political Philosophy*, London, 1785.
Parliamentary Acts, Vict., London, 1884.
Prothero, G.W. (ed.), *Select Statutes and other Constitutional Documents illustrative of the Reigns of Elizabeth and James I*, 4th edn, Oxford, 1913.
Pugh, M., *State and Society: British Political and Social History 1870–1992*, London, 1994.

Read, D., *England 1868–1914: The Age of Urban Democracy*, London, 1979.

Robson, W., *Justice and Administrative Law*, London, 1928.

Stansfeld, J., *On the Failure of the Contagious Diseases Acts, as proved by the official evidence submitted to the select committee of the House of Commons*, London, 1881.

Vincent, A., and Plant, R., *Philosophy, Politics and Citizenship: The Life and Thought of the British Idealists*, Oxford, 1983.

Williams, G., and Ramsden, J.A., *Ruling Britannia: A Political History of Britain 1688–1988*, London, 1990.

Biographical Notes on the Editor and Contributors

The Author

Albert Venn Dicey was born at Claybrook Hall, near Lutterworth, Leicestershire, on 4 February 1835. He was educated at King's College School, London, and Balliol College, Oxford, where he obtained a first class in classical moderations in 1856 and in *Literae humaniores* in 1858. In 1860 Dicey was elected to a fellowship at Trinity College, Oxford, and in 1861 he studied for the bar at the Inner Temple, and then practised at the bar until 1882. As a result of his marriage in 1872 he forfeited his fellowship at Trinity. In 1882 Dicey was elected to the Vinerian professorship of English Law in The University of Oxford. He held this chair, attached to the fellowship of All Souls College, for twenty-seven years. Dicey established himself as a great expert on constitutional history when in 1885 he published his *Introduction to the Study of the Law of the Constitution*, universally recognised as a major classic on the British constitutional system. Dicey's other publications include: *A Treatise on the Rules for the Selection of the Parties to an Action* (1870); *The Law of Domicile, as a Branch of the Law of England, Stated in the Form of Rules* (1879); *England's Case Against Home Rule* (1886); *Letters on Unionist Delusions* (1887); *A Leap in the Dark* (1893); *A Digest of the Law of England with Reference to the Conflict of Laws* (1896); *Lectures on the Relation between Law and Public Opinion in England during the Nineteenth Century* (1905); *A Fool's Paradise* (1913); (with Robert Rait) *Thoughts on the Union between England and Scotland* (1920). Dicey died in Oxford on 7 April 1922.

Lord Plant of Highfield

Raymond Plant, PhD, DLitt; Professor of Jurisprudence and Legal Philosophy, King's College, London, since 2001. Life Peer cr 1992. Professor of Politics, 1979–94, Pro-Chancellor, 1996–9, University of Southampton. Master, St Catherine's College, Oxford, 1994–9. Chair: Labour Party Commn Electoral Systems, 1991–93. President: Acad. of Learned Socs in Social Scis, 2000–1. Hon. Fellow: St Catherine's College, Oxford; Harris Manchester College, Oxford; Cardiff University. Publications: *Hegel*, 1974; *Community and Ideology*, 1974; *Political Philosophy and Social Welfare*, 1981; *Philosophy, Politics and Citizenship*, 1984; *Modern Political Thought*, 1991; *Politics, Theology and History*, 2000.

The Editor

Peter Raina read Modern History at St Catherine's College, Oxford, received his MA at Clark University (USA), his D Phil from Warsaw University. He has been a Research Fellow at the Osteuropa-Institut, Free University, Berlin; a Visiting Fellow at the Centre of International Studies, Faculty of History, Cambridge University, at the Centre for International Studies, London School of Economics and Political Science; Research Associate, St Catherine's College, Oxford; Senior Research Associate, Balliol College, Oxford; Honorary Member of the High Table and Senior Common Room member, Christ Church, Oxford. He is a Life member, Clare Hall, Cambridge and Knight Companion Grand Cross of the Order of St Stanislas (founded 1765). Peter Raina is the author of a number of books, which include: *George Macaulay Trevelayan*, *The Constitutions of New Democracies in Europe* and *Bishop George Bell.*

Index